TO.
ELUIN & JAN,
EXPECT
TO
WIN!
Bob.
Wieland
LUKE 1:37

"For nothing is impossible with God" (Luke 1:37)

ONE
STEP
AT
A
TIME

THE REMARKABLE TRUE STORY OF BOB WIELAND

by BOB WIELAND

as told to Sarah Nichols

ZondervanPublishingHouse

Grand Rapids, Michigan

A Division of HarperCollinsPublishers

One Step at a Time
Copyright © 1989 by Bob Wieland and Sarah Nichols

Requests for information should be addressed to:
Zondervan Publishing House Grand Rapids, Michigan 49530

Library of Congress Cataloging-in-Publication Data

Wieland, Bob.
  One step at a time : the remarkable true story of Bob Wieland / by
Bob Wieland as told to Sarah Nichols.
      p. cm.
  ISBN 0-310-51640-4
  1. Wieland, Bob. 2. Christian biography—United States.
3. Vietnamese Conflict, 1961–1975—Veterans—United States.
4. Veterans—United States—Biography. 5. Physically handicapped—
United States—Biography. 6. Walking—United States. I. Nichols,
Sarah. II. Title.
BR1725.W448A3   1989
917.304'927–dc20   89–16620
[B]   CIP

The names of some of the people described in this book have been changed to protect their privacy. Some characters are composite sketches and some dialogue has been dramatized.

Unless otherwise noted, all Scripture references are taken from the *Holy Bible: New International Version* (North American Edition), copyright © 1973, 1978, 1984 by the International Bible Society. Used by permission of Zondervan Bible Publishers.

Printed in the United States of America

96 97 98 99 00 /❖ DH / 12 11 10 9 8 7 6

CONTENTS

To every person who has contributed to my life, especially my parents, Bill and Ida Wieland; and to everyone who contributed in any way to make possible the Walk Across America to feed the spiritually and physically hungry people of the United States. You know who you are, and I thank you!

Thanks to my wife, Jackey Wieland, and to Harry Sneider, Margaret Harvey, Marshall Cardiff, Isaac Ruiz, and Tom Da Mota, who gave their all to help make the journey possible.

My special gratitude to Dennis Cooper who saved my life in Vietnam and to Jerome Lubeno and the approximately 58,000 brave men and women who lost their lives fighting and dying for their country.

Most of all I dedicate this book to the glory and honor of the living Lord Jesus Christ.

PART ONE
PREPARATION

1

WAR, REAL WAR

My first day in Vietnam. I stood in a compound, which was surrounded by barbed wire strung with Dr Pepper, Coke, and 7-Up cans. I grew curious. "Why the cans?" I asked the sergeant.

He explained, "There're pebbles in the cans in case there's a human-wave attack."

Slowly it sunk in. When the Viet Cong rushed up against the barbed wire, the cans made an unmistakable noise. "When you hear it," Sarge continued, "you got about forty-five seconds to defend your life."

"Hold it, Sarge. Am I going back to the U.S. alive?"

"Don't count on it!"

I felt the pit of my stomach sink.

In training at Fort Sam Houston in San Antonio, Texas, I was given two choices. I could serve my country as a cook or as a medic. I knew I didn't know how to cook. So, since I liked to help people and care for them, I chose to be a medic. I had no idea what I was getting into.

So on April 1, 1969, I landed in Nam ready to help—or so I thought. I was stationed at Cu Chi, one of the base camps for the Army's Twenty-fifth Infantry Division. Before that moment, standing around with a hundred soldiers, mostly there for the first time on orientation, I had thought, *Hey, Cu Chi's a big base camp, like a small city within a city. I'm safe here.* But my sense of security was fleeting.

Cu Chi was built in the area the Vietnamese called Dong Zu, on heavily hit terrain, defoliated by Agent Orange, and considered some of the most devastated land in the history of warfare. Cu Chi, about twenty-five miles northwest of Saigon, lay between the strategic road and river approaches to the capital. Bordered to the north by the Saigon River, the area was continually assaulted by the Viet Cong. Their Saigon-area headquarters, complete with two hospitals and training depots, was nearby. And from what we could tell, an abandoned rubber plantation was a constant source of rocket and mortar attacks.

The hills surrounding the base were steep, rugged, and covered with deep jungle underbrush. A little farther north were the eerie Ho Bo Woods, near the village of Phu My Hung.

My first official duty in Nam was to carry off the bodies of some dead soldiers and to load them into black bags. I had never dealt much with death. Again, I felt uneasy.

After the first three days of basic orientation in Cu Chi, the call came for us to move out.

On one of my first missions, fifty-four of us piled into nine choppers, six guys to a chopper. Since the choppers had no doors, we sat with our legs dangling out. As we flew down the Saigon River, the gunners opened up the machine guns full blast, firing at the tree line.

I said to myself, *Hey! This isn't a movie. It's for real!* When the helicopters came down a few feet from the ground, we were told to jump out. What a surprise! I had thought we were going to land and just step out of the chopper onto the ground. Instead, with the propellers still going, everybody leaped into the rice paddies—a soft landing in a foot or two of water. The gunners in the choppers kept firing at the tree line; then, without warning, the choppers left.

Knee deep in polluted, smelly water, we trudged toward the tree line. All of a sudden bullets came whizzing over my head.

Then it wasn't just the war that was real—the *battle* was real. Until that day, all my training had seemed like make-believe. In basic training I had been taught that as long as you crouched lower than four feet, you wouldn't get hit. So, there in the rice paddies with the Viet Cong firing at us, I hit the ground and lay in the water; water insects and all kinds of weird-looking bugs crawled over me.

Then someone shouted my name; somebody'd been hit. Before I got to the wounded soldier, he died. Soon, a couple of other guys were loaded up in black plastic bags and carried out.

The next thing I knew, we were fighting hot and heavy—for our lives. After six or seven hours, two F-4 Navy Phantom jets flew in. The men around me were as excited as little kids. Those babies flew in low to the ground and dropped straight down. Their flight pattern was impressive. The power of the jets seemed to surge through my own body. After the bombs were dropped, the pilots flew straight up and out. As the bombs exploded, we cheered as if we'd seen Superman.

Then the firing stopped; the jets were miles away. Full of confidence, we started to walk toward the trees to see how many of the enemy had been killed.

Suddenly, the Viet Cong popped up from their deep tunnels and resumed their attack. Our eyeballs nearly popped out of our heads. The Viet Cong had simply escaped underground into dusty, red-earth tunnels and waited for the jets to leave.

At base camp, some of the soldiers said the tunnels of Cu Chi were almost impenetrable, having survived the assault of the most high-tech war machines in the world. But you never believe what you hear until you witness it firsthand.

Before long I acquired the nickname "Herc" (short for Hercules) because I looked like a professional weight lifter. At the time I weighed 205 pounds and was in good shape—the picture of health. Being strong, I could backpack the other men's ammunition and hike for miles. To me this was another workout, a good way to stay fit. Besides, I figured, carrying those packs would make me a better soldier. Actually, I think I carried the ammo packs to compensate for what I felt I hadn't been able to accomplish as a medic.

The truth was, I knew I was in way over my head. Eight weeks of medical training hadn't prepared me for the injuries I faced. Working on Susie, the Red Cross doll, is a lot different from working on a soldier with his arm blown off. One guy had been hit in the stomach and his guts were hanging out. Still alive, he said, "Can you help me?"

He was in shock. I said to myself, *How am I gonna fix this?* I had no idea what to do. Looking back, it's hard to understand how I could have walked into the battlefield so ill-prepared.

Preparation had always been a key word for me. In high school, I was never a kid who wandered aimlessly around with no plans or goals. No, I had a dream, and I did everything in my power to make that dream come true.

My goal was to become a pitcher for the Philadelphia Phillies or New York Mets. This life-long dream of a career in pro ball had started in childhood and was fueled by my father, a real-estate salesman, by my dad's father, who had played semi-pro baseball in Ironwood, Michigan, and by my mother, a homemaker who was always there for me. She fixed breakfasts and brown-bag lunches and was always waiting for me when I came home from school. Although I lacked many other advantages, I had plenty of love from two dedicated, hard-working parents who loved each other very much. My dad prided himself on working three jobs to make ends meet so my mom could stay home and care for me.

Those three important grown-ups in my life had always encouraged me and cheered me on. My dad and grandfather played catch with me; they taught me how to pitch and hit. They also taught me that sportsmanship was the most important aspect of any sport; how the game was played was more important than winning. I never forgot that. I was always competing against myself, doing the best I could, achieving the highest possible standard of performance. I found that when I did my best, the rest took care of itself.

By the time I was twenty-three, I had played approximately a hundred sanctioned baseball games and had pitched three no-hitters. To prepare for the love of my life, baseball, I practiced long and hard. I worked out with weights two to three times a week, and once in a while in the summer I enjoyed swimming and playing golf.

During one Wisconsin winter, in fact, I counted that I had ice skated at least 270 times; I had played approximately 740 games of basketball and 30 games of football; I had practiced football 720 hours, bowled 1,000 games, and played 200 games of squash. From my viewpoint, all this activity was not unusual. As far as I knew, all the athletes in my school and across the nation loved sports the way I did.

My parents never missed a basketball game, not even a practice. My classmates teased me because my mom and dad were like shadows, always in the background—watching me and cheering for me.

And their perseverance paid off. Around the time I pitched a complete game with a total of nineteen strikeouts, which broke a league record, scouts from the Phillies expressed an interest in signing me up. My dream was finally coming true.

But about that same time, I received another offer I couldn't refuse—my draft notice.

By the time I left for Vietnam, proud to serve my country, I thought, as my family did, that I'd be home within a year to play professional baseball. I dreamed of the day they'd be at the airport waiting to cheer me home.

Within weeks of my arrival in Nam, days and nights began to run together, as life took on one sole purpose: to get ready for search-and-destroy missions, to go on ambush patrols, and to patch up the wounded.

There was no time to play cards, no energy to think of home, family, or friends. Still, sometimes when I ate my c-rations—hard candy, beans, reconstituted scrambled eggs, sometimes rancid peanut butter, jelly crackers, ham, and bacon—I'd remember my mom's homemade cooking: steak, fish, fried chicken, potatoes, and pie. I would get so hungry for her cooking that I could almost smell the apple-cinnamon pie in the oven.

Nor was there much time to get acquainted with the men in my company, since soldier after soldier either died, got wounded, or was transferred. Friends were important to surviving in Vietnam, however. Being a medic, I had the opportunity to get to know my commanding officer, six-foot, blond-haired, blue-eyed Lieutenant Jim Sylvester from Seattle. I watched him closely and admired his style, always sensitive to the needs of his men.

I spent time with a young man named Jerome Lubeno; we were both from Wisconsin and loved to compare notes, especially about sports and Wisconsin summers. As a student at the University of Wisconsin in Madison, Jerome had been a first-rate competitive swimmer. He looked like a California surfer with his sandy-blond hair and lean 175-pound body. He hadn't decided on a career. All he wanted to do was to go home, finish college, get married someday, and settle down. Our common goal was to serve our country and get back to Wisconsin—alive.

I also enjoyed the company of lanky, dark-haired Dennis Cooper from Missouri. A happy, enthusiastic guy, Dennis got along with everybody. He was a born-again Christian who had received his draft notice the day he'd found out his wife was pregnant. Dennis was already in Nam when his son was born. He told me his mom got down on her knees, everyday without fail, and prayed for his safe return.

Then there was Hopkins, the radio man from Detroit, and David Denier, the point man who had the courage to take on every assignment no matter how dangerous.

But in spite of friends and dreams of returning home, I fought back waves of exhaustion and fatigue. Raw fear, mixed with the smell of dusty, dirty, bone-tired bodies, pervaded the camp; we were so tired sometimes that we couldn't even eat. And the war took its toll on more than just us soldiers.

My first trip to the nearby village of Cu Chi horrified me. The children—emaciated, hungry, fighting with one another for scraps of rotten GI garbage. Their need was so overwhelming and I felt so helpless. Wasn't there anything I could do to help them?

I was particularly drawn to one baby, just skin and bones. Her mother approached me with an outstretched hand, and my first instinct was to turn and run away. I can still see the baby's face covered with sores that oozed pus. Her expression and dark eyes mirrored the anguish I felt. The mother drew close, and I gave her the only medical supplies I had—some aspirin and soap.

When I get home I've got to help these children, I thought. *No one should have to live like this.* Other mothers were soon calling out for medicine to heal the sores on their own sick and dying children.

Soon a crowd of children, mostly boys, surrounded me, begging for chocolate candy and bits of food. I couldn't resist, and for one second I laid down my rifle to see what I had in my pockets. I had hardly turned my back before the rifle was gone. *What kind of a soldier am I?* I wondered. *What am I going to tell my commanding officer? Some kid stole my gun?* I headed back to the base, apprehensive and discouraged.

On the way I saw an emaciated six-year-old boy leading a huge water buffalo. The animal looked friendly enough at first, but when I approached, the animal had a silent, warning look in his eye: Keep a safe distance. To this day I remember the effects of war reflected in the eyes of that little boy with the water buffalo and the hunger and desperation reflected in that sick baby's eyes.

Back at camp, I discovered, to my puzzlement, that my rifle had mysteriously returned.

June 14, 1969. As far as I can remember, it started out like any other day in the jungle, but for one thing: a fog of danger hovered even closer in the stifling, humid air. Was it a premonition or just my imagination?

We were ordered out on patrol that morning. Before we left I reminded Jerome that I had only nine-and-a-half months left to serve in Vietnam. "Then it's back home to the ball field," I said. I could feel my hand in that leather glove. I could picture myself on the pitcher's mound, throwing a no-hitter for the Phillies. Jerome smiled. His tour of duty would end before mine, and he too was eager to return home and get on with his life.

As our patrol moved toward the woods, I still had the uneasy feeling that we were heading into danger. Suddenly, the usual loud hum of insects, birds, and animals fell silent, and we were pelted by a monsoon rainstorm. We walked and walked and walked. It stopped raining, and I started to doze a little as I walked. Then, suddenly, we were drenched by another downpour.

Maybe I was losing touch with reality, like going to an amusement park and looking at fun-house mirrors. For us it was a constant fight to hold onto reality and adjust to the environment and the war.

As I moved stealthily through the jungle, fighting exhaustion, wanting to rest, I thought about the war. It was so real—yet so unreal. Most of us were just eighteen- to twenty-two years old, thrown together from the streets of Milwaukee, San Diego, Rochester, or wherever.

I looked around, warily. Sometimes it seemed even the trees had eyes. No matter how quiet I tried to be, the underbrush crunched noisily under my feet. I tried to step carefully, knowing that even a little noise could be deadly.

Death—maybe that was what was hanging in the air. I was learning too much about it, too soon. My grandfather William had died from a heart attack when I was in high school, but he had been ill for some time and had lived a full life. But these men all around me were still young. They hadn't tasted life. Some were friends, and I tried my best to shut off the deep pain, grief, and sorrow I felt. I had to stay strong and keep on going. A combat medic had to hang tough, along with the rest of the men. We were a team.

As I walked, I thought of the time Hopkins, the radio man, had captured some Viet Cong who were yelling and screaming in their native tongue as they lay on the ground. The person in charge said, "Well, let's call in a dust-off helicopter to pick them up and carry them back to camp."

Another soldier said, "Let's dust 'em off right here." He put his gun on automatic and sent sixteen rounds into a dying enemy's neck. His head rolled down the hill like a bowling ball. It was all I could do to keep from vomiting.

Then I thought about the first time I'd been hit. A soldier behind me had stepped on a hand grenade, and the compression sent me flying. My back was hot with the shrapnel, which stung like bees. My shirt was bloody, but I figured I was okay;

so I kept on going, trying to help another soldier who'd been hit by a booby-trap. Soon he said, "Hey, you've been hit too." All we could do was to try to comfort each other. I was not only concerned about my own injuries, but I knew that wherever there is one booby trap, others are nearby. Medics had to be careful when helping wounded soldiers not to step on booby traps.

Sometimes it was even hard to know who was shooting at whom. Some of the Vietnamese were notorious for switching sides. I thought of one man in particular who had been captured by the Americans and was now fighting on our side. His name was Ming Dong Zu Ling Wong. It didn't take long before we nicknamed him Ralph.

Three months ago Ralph had been an enemy, doing his best to kill us. Now he liked the American Army because the officers gave him clean clothes and two hundred dollars a month. He was five-foot-three, weighed about 115 pounds, and was a martial arts expert. I wondered where Ralph was now when we needed him. He could recognize dangers that we were often oblivious to.

As I walked, I realized it all was getting to me; so much had happened in such a short time. On top of it all, like my comrades, I was worn out from trying to project an image of superior strength. As I looked around cautiously, I was sick of the whole thing. And that sense of uneasiness in the pit of my stomach grew stronger.

I had forgotten what it was like to have a good night's sleep. On this June day in particular I was past the point of exhaustion. I was hungry and obsessively longing for fried chicken, mashed potatoes, pie, and cold milk. I thought about my first day in camp ten weeks earlier when I had craved a drink of milk. I ran for the wax carton like a man chasing a mirage in the desert. I gulped it quickly and spit it out—warm and sour. Yuck! *Cold milk*, I thought, *a mirage in the jungle!*

I forced myself to keep on going as I, and the fifteen other soldiers, cut through the jungle. Lieutenant Jim Sylvester too sensed the impending danger and warned us to be wary as we drew closer to the menacing Ho Bo Woods.

But it was too late. We had already marched unknowingly

into a daisy-leaf mine field. There was a sudden explosion. I heard the familiar cries, "Doc, Doc," and I knew one of those desperate voices was Jerome's. I had to get there quick. Running in long strides, I headed for the voice. I would save my Wisconsin buddy!

2

ALIVE!

DOA—dead on arrival—that's what the hospital report said. Yet the staff tried anyway. I'd lost virtually all my blood and received nearly eight quarts of transfusions. I wasn't breathing on my own, but with the help of a tracheotomy.

When I woke up, doped and groggy, an intravenous bag dripped life into my arm—liquid breakfast, lunch, and dinner. Shock, the mercy of God, and a quarter grain of morphine every four hours dulled my perception of pain, even of reality.

Bit by bit, piece by piece, I learned from the other wounded men in my company what had happened. Running to help Jerome and the other wounded men, I had stepped on a booby-trapped eighty-two-millimeter mortar round—powerful enough to put a tank out of commission. I discovered Jerome hadn't made it.

As soon as I was able to speak I asked the doctor on duty, "Tell me, Doc, how long did I have, fifteen minutes?"

He replied, "More like fifteen seconds."

"Wow! It's a miracle!" I said.

But there were complications, as my temperature hovered between 105 and 106 degrees most of the time. Between the hot weather, the humidity, and my high fever, I had a terrific thirst and drank gallons of water. Even being packed in ice didn't bring my temperature down, and the doctors suspected I had malaria.

Accompanying the fever and the morphine were the nightmares. I saw exploding body parts, blood splashing on the ground. I heard the dying cries of my comrades, and then the terrible silence that followed. I remembered the stench of gangrene and would wake up sweating with fear. Then I'd drift off again, and the discordant cacophony of dying voices would start all over.

During my waking moments I heard the voices of doctors and nurses and bits and pieces of their bedside conversations. They still weren't sure I would make it.

My day-to-day survival was a miracle indeed. And at times I felt as if I were in a hand-to-hand battle with Satan, who was trying to kill me, discourage me, and convince me that life was over. At other times, and ever so slowly, I began to understand that the God who saved my life on the battlefield that day is full of love, compassion, wisdom, and grace. *He must have something in mind for me,* I thought. *There must be something I can do. This can't be the end of my athletic career!*

As a sophomore at the University of Wisconsin at LaCrosse, some guys from Campus Crusade for Christ had visited the apartment I shared with seven other students. Called the "Bat Cave," the apartment was named after the old "Batman" television show—and also after the live creatures that occupied the attic. The visitors witnessed to us, and that night I knelt by my bed and talked to God—for the first time—as if He were my best friend. When I invited Him into my life, I felt a deep peace and joy.

But in the three intervening years, my enthusiasm had dwindled and my peace had lessened. Now, on the brink of death, that peace returned. When I first awoke to life in that hospital, drugged and groggy as I was, I felt an odd sense of joy and contentment. At that moment, I was deeply grateful to be AOA—alive on arrival. I tasted how precious each moment of life is. I said a silent prayer of thanks, for life and for salvation.

So I realized that my spiritual life was intact, if not strengthened. But there was something else I began to realize—ever so slowly. From the waist down I was carefully covered with a white sheet. It was days before I knew why.

In one of my more lucid moments I wrote to my parents. I thought I should break the news to them before a hospital representative did.

Dear Mom and Dad:

I'm in the hospital. Everything is going to be O.K. The people here are taking good care of me. It won't be that much of an adjustment. Please don't worry about me. Maybe I'll help you out in real estate.

Love,
Bob

P.S. I think I lost my legs!

I remember the moment the truth first dawned on me. I glanced down at the white sheet and slid my hands cautiously down to touch my legs. There was nothing there. Pulling the sheet to one side, I looked down and saw huge bandages wrapping my upper thighs and the long, bare expanse of white sheet. As I lay there, before I could react to my discovery, a nurse came in to give me a shot to put me to sleep. *I'll deal with this later*, I promised myself as I quickly drifted off to another world.

Later I was told that the mortar I'd stepped on had blown my legs in one direction, my body in the other. Half of my blood had poured into the earth like rain. I was on the final countdown when an unidentified soldier from my company got me to a helicopter that had been rerouted at the last moment. I was alive—though no longer six feet tall and weighing 205 pounds. I was two feet, ten-and-a-half inches tall, weighing 87 pounds.

On the third day in the hospital I was rolled into surgery, where the doctor folded the skin over my stumps, and two days later I was shipped to a hospital outside Tokyo for more treatment and tests to determine whether I had malaria. At least that was a disease that could be treated.

The tests came back positive, and the malaria shots—in the

buttocks with what looked like horse needles—quickly began
to work. Within three days my temperature went down to 101
degrees. I learned firsthand that sleep and time are great
healers. Once my fever went down, the nightmares were less
frequent and were mixed with images of Wisconsin—playing
ball with my grandfather. Awake or asleep, I sometimes
dreamed I was pitching for the Phillies. We were always
winning, and I could hear the fans yelling. Often I was
pitching my first professional no-hitter, feeling good, real good.
But then I would wake up and see my bandaged stumps.
Whom was I kidding? Surely it was time for a nurse to come
and give me a shot to put me to sleep.

One morning I woke early with a new throbbing relentless
pain in my stumps—a sign, said the doctor, that I was
beginning to heal. The fire from the fever had been replaced
with an itching soreness that consumed me.

And with that so-called healing pain came a new wave of
anguish that momentarily flooded me. Was my life as an
athlete over at twenty-two? The question haunted me and the
answer seemed to be yes. But that yes never really took root in
my mind. I knew that what *seems* to be and what *is* are two
different things. As I lay in that hospital and stared at the
ceiling day after day I determined that my dream was not going
to end just because I had no legs. So I had to overcome an
obstacle? I'd done it before. I could do it again.

I promised myself one thing: With God's help I could and
would overcome all obstacles. In my heart and soul I was an
athlete. Surely there was a sport out there I could compete in.

It was obvious by the way doctors and nurses treated me that
they thought of me as "handicapped." So, almost in spite of
them, I determined to think of myself as an able-bodied
individual. I became so independent that I even insisted on
cleaning my own wounds, which was one big challenge
because of the scabs—and the smell.

After two weeks in Japan I thought I was strong enough to
get out of bed, which meant that I had convinced the doctors
and nurses to take me outside for some fresh air. I'll admit that
it took me forty-five minutes to get out of bed and into the
wheelchair, and each move I made increased the excruciating

pain. But I did it. A nurse wheeled me out into the hot summer air. Though oppressive, it was delightful. I took three breaths of it and fell asleep, exhausted. When I woke up I was back in bed. So much for my first outing.

Soon after my first outing I was strapped into a traveling litter. One of a planeload of wounded men, I was going home. Triple-stacked in a yellow school bus, minus its seats, there were three inches between me and the man above me. This was no air-conditioned school bus, but I didn't mind. I was going stateside—home!

The commanding officer's voice shouted loud and clear, "Let's get the show on the road!" and the troops started to move.

Though I was leaving Japan, I was, in a larger sense, leaving Vietnam. I was returning to the U.S.—*alive* if not kicking.

3

PHILADELPHIA, BUT *NOT* THE PHILLIES

Aboard a C-5 hospital plane, the long trip, halfway around the world, didn't seem to drag. For those twelve to eighteen hours, the U.S.A. was my idea of heaven! When we touched down, I was in glory.

After a brief stop in Fort Dix, New Jersey, on July 17, we reached our final destination—Valley Forge Army Hospital outside Philadelphia. To think—after all those years of hoping to spend a summer in Philadelphia, this wasn't exactly what I had in mind!

Valley Forge was a hospital for amputees, staffed by some of the finest specialists in the country, including Captain Craig Roberts, my attending physician; Colonel Lanoue, head of orthopedics; and Colonel Duffer, head administrator and chief of staff.

When I was wheeled inside the doors, I knew I wasn't staying there for long—because I had a goal. In six weeks I was going to be out and back on my own. One overly eager nurse tried to comb my hair. I explained I would do it myself, thank you. Then she tried to button my shirt. I said I appreciated her help, but I could button my own shirt. Not to be discouraged, she tried to feed me. "Wait a minute," I said. "Do you think I'm helpless? I really can take care of myself." Maybe she'd been used to working with other guys who didn't want to return to a normal life.

In Valley Forge I learned how to take care of myself and I made some good friends. First, there was Eddie Henry, a curly-haired man in the bed next to me. Being from the local area, Eddie received visits from as many as a dozen different women—blondes, brunettes, and redheads of all shapes and sizes. I always knew when it was 6:00 A.M. and time to get up, because that's when Ed turned his radio up full blast. Radios seemed to form the backdrop for those days, full of noise and Janis Joplin tunes.

I got to know some of the other double amputees in my ward, and our mutual humor and caring helped us adjust to our situation. Lying in bed one day, I came up with what I thought was a pretty good idea. "Hey, guys, why don't we get jobs in Palm Springs, modeling Bermuda shorts? Or maybe we could get jobs as driving instructors!"

Once I said, "You know, teaching people about being professional amputees might not be such a bad idea." That time I was only half joking, and the guys seemed to realize it. I think it got a few thinking.

One morning a doctor and a therapist, who held a five-pound weight, approached my bed. "Hey, Bob," said the therapist, "see what you can do with this."

Mustering all the strength in my eighty-seven pound body, I couldn't sit up in bed and do a simple triceps extension. I thought I saw a look of concern on their faces, which only made me more determined.

"Hey, don't worry, Doc," I said. "Someday I may break a weight-lifting record!"

The doctor quickly jotted some notes on my chart.

What a shock—the first time I saw myself in a full-length mirror and realized what I looked like minus 118 pounds. I had worked hard to put on all that muscle; now I'd have to start all over again.

Those days I traveled mostly on my stomach, on a gurney decorated with Snoopy dressed as the World War One Flying Ace. My new nickname was "Cadillac Jack," maybe because Eddie Henry and I discovered we could race down the halls and huge ramps. There were no elevators at Valley Forge. It was the greatest place to race, and we agreed that the winner would win five bucks!

My gurney had big tires in the front and little tires in the back, and I soon learned that by pushing the big tires forward and quickly reversing, I could make the gurney stand up and do a wheelie. What a way to freak out the nurses—who didn't appreciate my sense of humor!

At times the emotional and physical pain tried to overwhelm me. As an antidote I managed to stay busy and keep moving. Action and new interests occupied all of my available time; I stopped thinking and feeling anything that wasn't positive. I knew if I allowed negative thoughts and emotions to poison my mind, I'd never adjust.

Seeds of dreams and plans started to take root in my thoughts. I'd finish college and then teach physical education. And maybe weight lifting would be the sport in which the crowds would cheer me on. Yeh, I'd go for it.

Though I had sensed God's presence when I first awoke after the explosion, now that awareness had quickly and drastically disappeared. My positive thoughts were more sheer willpower than dependence on or awareness of God. It would be years before I thought of God again as Someone who might want my attention.

As standard procedure (or maybe because the doctors thought I was overly optimistic), I had to visit the hospital psychiatrist.

The gray-haired serious-looking doctor sat behind his desk, peering at me through his glasses. His first question caught me off guard. "Why are you smiling? Are you trying to hide the bitterness you feel for losing your legs?"

"No, man, I'm smiling because I'm happy; I'm glad I'm alive. If it'll make you feel better, I'll frown." So I frowned.

He countered, "Why are you frowning? Is it because you're unhappy that you lost your legs?"

I shrugged. What did this guy want? I was running out of facial expressions. The rest of the interview didn't get any better. When it was over, I said, "Hey, Doc, if you ever need any help, come on down and see me. I'm in Ward 4-C-D."

To keep busy and get in shape, from 6:00 A.M. until curfew I participated in almost every physical therapy and activity session in the hospital. I frequently went down and checked in at the Red Cross Center to find out what was going on in the way of activities.

As we got further along in our recuperation, the Red Cross used to load us onto the hospital bus and take us to outside events—boxing matches and basketball games in Philadelphia and New Jersey, and to concerts to see Ray Charles, Marilyn McCoo, and the Fifth Dimension. I remember especially admiring Ray Charles—having overcome his blindness. He was an inspiration to me. He had never let his disability affect his professional goals.

One evening we even had a police escort to the Ed Sullivan Show in New York, where we appreciated seeing Robbie Robertson and the Band in action. In those days veterans were treated like royalty. We were introduced as Vietnam veterans, and a spotlight was usually aimed in our direction. The American Red Cross played an important part in my recovery, and I am grateful to the organization and their volunteers— even to this day. As time went by I also learned to appreciate the camaraderie in the hospital, among the men, staff, and volunteers.

During my stay at Valley Forge my diet changed considerably. I left behind the intravenous tubes and the soft foods, and was allowed to eat a regular diet. I soon regained some of the weight I had lost. It seemed in no time I was off the gurney and into a wheelchair. Then I looked forward to graduating to artificial legs.

Valley Forge Hospital was known for its state-of-the-art artificial legs. I was so excited. Just maybe I could walk fast again—like I used to.

Finally, the day came when I was fitted for legs called stubbies. At first I was uncomfortable. They resembled pontoons and were *very* artificial. With my stubbies attached I was now three-foot-nine-inches tall. I don't know what I expected from my new legs. Perhaps I'd thought life would return to normal—pre-June 14.

I enjoyed walking outside, feeling the warmth of the sun on my back, taking in the sight and smell of the flowers growing on the well-kept hospital grounds. But within a short time I realized using artificial legs was nothing like the real thing. It wasn't that they didn't work or that I couldn't maneuver them. Being an athlete, I had a good sense of equilibrium and could walk pretty well within a short period of time. I simply could move much faster on the gurney or wheelchair than on the legs.

Soon after that there was another eagerly anticipated day. I had talked to my parents often, but late in July they were coming to visit. "Great," I said; I wanted to see them. But as I waited for them to walk through the door, I began to wonder about how they would accept my injury. As I discovered in Vietnam, hearing something isn't the same as seeing it with your very own eyes. How would my injury affect their lives? As far as I knew, they still had their hearts set on me playing pro ball.

My parents had looked forward to the day I'd find a wife and have children, including at least one boy to bounce on my dad's knee and to play ball with him. Would I ever find a wife, and if I did, would I have children?

All of a sudden Mom walked into the room. She hadn't changed a bit. Dad looked great too. With a warm and encouraging smile, he said, "Hey, Bob, how you doing?"

"Great, Dad!"

With tears in her eyes, my mom reached down and hugged me. "What can we do to make you more comfortable?"

"Hey! I'm doing great. Don't worry. I'll show you around this place."

Dad reached for the handles of my wheelchair as if he had done it all his life, and he started to push it. I knew my need for independence would be the hardest thing for them to understand. So I thanked Dad, but I rolled myself down the corridor.

Throughout the day we reminisced, and I told them my plans for the future—getting a college degree in physical education and then teaching, competing in weight-lifting contests. They were encouraging, and I was again reminded of how grateful I was for them.

One evening soon after my parents' visit, my buddy Eddie Henry and I were hanging out in a different part of the hospital—cruising on our gurneys. When we rolled outside for a breath of air, Eddie said, "Hey, Bob, do you hear that?"

"Yeah, let's track it down, see where the music's coming from." In a moment we were off on a new adventure.

We discovered the music was coming from the NCO Club on the third floor. We also discovered that the club doors were locked. "The fire escape," one of us said, and we headed for the staircase that went up the outside of the brick building. My weight lifting was paying off. We climbed up those stairs like two monkeys after bananas. The party-goers laughed when they heard us knock on the window. We partied well that night. It felt good to be young and still alive.

The next day six of my buddies and I decided to attend a peace rally near Philadelphia. We didn't know what we were getting into; the rally was anything but peaceful. In some ways it was like a circus: vendors selling hot dogs and popcorn to the milling crowd. Protest signs were everywhere: Gays for Peace, Lesbians for Peace, Black Panthers for Peace. We searched the crowd for one Vietnam disabled veterans' group. None.

Some of my buddies had dressed in their Nam uniforms, which made us like prey for the vultures. "Murderers," some people began to shout. "Baby killers, go home." The cries were directed at us. What were they talking about? We were home! My blood began to simmer. How could these Americans turn on us? We'd been serving our country—their country. We'd lost limb—and nearly life—for our country's freedom. Why were they shaking fists at us?

TV cameras quickly moved in and shot the noisy crowd. Eventually, we were given an opportunity to speak, and I was asked what being in Vietnam was like. With the cameras rolling, I simply stated the truth: There wasn't much time to sleep, and we existed in a technicolor nightmare.

What I didn't realize was that my statements would be

televised on Walter Cronkite's nighttime news. What a surprise awaited me back at the hospital, when I was ushered into the office of the administrator.

He got right to the point. "Specialist Wieland, do you realize you're still in the Army?"

"Yes sir!" I replied.

"Do you realize you've been giving away Army secrets and that you could be dishonorably discharged or court-martialed?"

Dishonorably discharged? Court-martialed? How? Why? All I'd said was we hadn't gotten much sleep.

He asked question after question, then let me go with a reprimand and a warning—not to do it again. I got the message loud and clear.

The next day things were back to normal; I was back at my workout routine, preparing for a new life. I gained back about forty-pounds—mostly muscle—during my time in the hospital. I thought I was beginning to look pretty good, and I was feeling pretty good. So one morning after therapy I talked my doctor into giving me a pass to leave the hospital for my first date. It took some talking. At first he was reluctant and quoted regulations. But eventually he agreed, and I took Joyce Jones, an attractive, blond therapist, to a movie. Joyce and I shared a few laughs, and my confidence soared. Though Joyce knew I was no knight in shining armor, she enjoyed me as I was—a regular guy who happened to be in a wheelchair, a man who appreciated her companionship.

To me, my first date was a sign that things were returning to normal. And other signs followed. Between August 1 and August 18, my strength quadrupled. My hard work and commitment began to pay off.

I'd had one immediate goal—to be out of that hospital. This time when I boarded the airplane, I wheeled myself down the aisle.

In his army uniform—
"An offer I couldn't
refuse."

Eighty-two mm. mortar
shell similar to the one
Bob stepped on in the
booby-trapped mine field
in Vietnam

Philadelphia but not the Phillies—Bob, weighing 87 pounds but in good spirits, recovering at Valley Forge Hospital near Philadelphia

Bob at 240 pounds—no longer a "light-weight"

Bob Wieland—in championship form

The planche—every bit as hard as it looks!

With Pat Boone at the Easter Seals Golf Tournament, 1983

Bob with Jan Scruggs, the motivating force behind the Vietnam Wall project

With Don Sutton of the Astros

Bob in training with Wendell Tyler of the L.A. Rams

4

BACK ON THE BLOCK

Mom and Dad were at the Milwaukee airport, eager to welcome me home—though home was not my immediate destination. The ambulance that picked me up drove me directly to the Wood Milwaukee Veterans' Hospital where I got checked out. I stayed there two weeks and was fitted for new, longer artificial legs. With these new legs I was now five-foot-ten. I was really coming up in the world!

While there, I learned to drive in the hospital parking lot. My instructor knew exactly what he was doing, but it took me a while to get the hang of hand controls—lurch, jerk, stop, and go. By the time I left, I had learned the trick of smooth sailing and was one step closer to freedom and an independent lifestyle.

Upon my release from the hospital, my parents drove me home in my dad's blue Oldsmobile. As we rolled along the freeway, Mom reminded me of my precarious entry into this world. Born two months early and with complications, I almost didn't make it. She said I was a survivor, and I figured that God must have something important He wanted me to do.

When we got home, Dad again reached for the handlebars of my wheelchair and started to push me up the sidewalk leading to the house. "Thanks, Dad, but I can do it," I said, and I gave those wheels a hard push. Inside, my mother started mothering me, waiting on me as if I were a child returned to her nest.

That first day, I realized, we had to have a family talk, though I did most of the talking. "I can manage," I said. "I can take care of myself, and it's important that I take care of myself. In the hospital I saw guys who wanted to be taken care of—and it's deadly. It'd be easy for me to slip back into your warm, loving care, but I'm not a kid. I'm not handicapped either; I'm an able-bodied man who happens to be missing two legs!"

What made them really sit up and take notice was my desire to drive a car. To the best of their ability, they understood. I knew what had happened to me had been devastating for both of them. Their only son, healthy and with aspirations to be a baseball pro, was now in a wheelchair, where athletic opportunities, to many people's way of thinking, were nonexistent. Yet I was healthy, able-bodied, an athlete—and a pretty fair weight lifter.

As our neighbors and friends came to visit that first day home, I realized that my greatest challenge would be to deal with people's reactions. Suddenly I was learning what generations of disabled people go through every day.

I looked at the faces of people I'd known all my life. As we sat together in the living room, after a few moments of awkward silence or polite conversation, I observed a variety of emotions and reactions—pity, sympathy, empathy, oversolicitousness. Some tried to pretend that nothing had changed. Soon, I excused myself to go to my bedroom and rest. It had been a long day, yes, but more than that, I just didn't know what to say.

On my second day home, my parents began to accept that I could take care of myself. Some things hadn't changed; Dad still liked to argue at the dinner table.

But it was great being back in my comfortable home, surrounded by my family and the memories of a secure childhood. Yet at times sadness, grief, and loss churned up from deep down inside me. I had left for Vietnam as a young kid, and a year later I'd come home as an adult. Maybe I was mourning the loss of my youth.

I thought of all the sporting events Mom, Dad, and I had attended—pro baseball in the summer, football in the fall, basketball in the winter. I remembered the first time we had rented a cabin at Little Saint Germain Lake during summer vacation. That fish I caught seemed to grow bigger every year.

More bits and pieces of the past came to mind: trading baseball cards with my friend David Wessel; Dad taking me to his work picnics and showing me off. Both my parents had always made me feel that I was somebody special, worth their time and attention, whether it was playing sports with me or baking me cookies.

My memories—especially of pitching a no-hitter at Humboldt Park near Milwaukee—were a mixed blessing. The thought of baseball prompted a deep pain of loss. My legs were gone, as was my dream of playing ball. Somehow, that reality was still not fully grown in my mind. Some mornings when I woke up from a sound sleep, I'd start to leap out of bed to get ready for baseball practice. Then looking down at where my legs used to be, I'd remember. Things had changed radically.

The new, longer artificial legs were a challenge. With crutches, both my arms were full. Even if I could manage two bags of groceries and two crutches, I had to think hard about how I was going to open the door.

Besides that, the legs didn't get me there fast enough—not nearly as fast as the wheelchair. The legs were relatively efficient, but I could go only as fast as the design of the equipment. There was only one way to take a step: throw my leg forward, lock it in place, then set my foot down. You could never step until the artificial knee locked in place. To walk three blocks would take maybe fifteen minutes—or so it seemed. In contrast, the wheelchair could go twenty to thirty miles per hour downhill.

During the winter I found out that it's not practical to push a wheelchair on ice or through snow, and after a few spills I promised myself I would go to California next winter.

Wisconsin winters weren't the only contrast to deal with after the tropical heat of Vietnam. The U.S. had changed. When I had left for Vietnam in early 1969, long hair on guys was just starting to come in. The hippie movement hadn't fully arrived yet, and by the time I returned it had all broken loose. Woodstock was the big event. In Philadelphia some of us vets had wanted to go up to Woodstock. But after our peace-demonstration disaster, maybe it was just as well that we couldn't get passes.

I was also surprised at the continuing racism in the U.S. In Vietnam, everyone was a brother. Being in life and death situations on a daily basis made us into a team—black, white, other races together. Now I noticed a lot of prejudice and hatred on both ends of the spectrum. Not only were the white people prejudiced, the blacks were too, perhaps because of the bondage that white society had forced on them.

While watching television with a neighbor of mine, he said, "Look at those niggers!" Right away I excused myself and went home. I've always listened carefully to what comes out of a person's mouth, since it tells me what's in that person's heart. No one talks that way if he or she isn't prejudiced. When I was a kid, someone I was close to had advised me not to play on a baseball team with a black coach and some black team members. That hurt. I'd always known it was wrong to think and feel that way, but the issue seemed even more important to me after what I'd been through in Nam.

In my home town there was even a lot of division within families. The news—in the paper or by word of mouth—was full of divorce, murder, and domestic violence. Family members who were supposed to be supporting each other were taking pot shots at each other—verbal if not physical. Again, I appreciated the stability in my parents' home.

Like any red-blooded American male, twenty-three years old, I wanted to date. It was ironic—during my college years when I could have picked from a number of women, I'd been so busy with sports that I had almost no time for dates. Now that I had time, the women were harder to find. Was my wheelchair a barrier?

Most men dream of being a prince charming, riding a white horse into a woman's life. I was riding a chrome wheelchair.

Susan Ruttin, one of my friends from college, agreed to go out with me—my first date since arriving home. I took her out for dinner, and we reminisced about old times. Just out of college, she was now enjoying her first teaching assignment. "What about you, Bob? What are your plans?" she asked, so warm and friendly, her blue eyes sparkling as she spoke.

"I'm going back to LaCrosse and taking four units toward a degree in physical education," I replied. "I want to teach."

"Super, that sounds terrific. You'll be a great teacher," she said. She had been a bubbly cheerleader, and she still was.

I had a wonderful time that evening, and at her front door I said, "Hey, what a great time! May I call you?"

"Sure," she said, "I really enjoyed it, just like old times."

Encouraged, I did call her—several times. We'd chat awhile; she was always friendly—and very busy. Eventually, I got the message.

But things weren't too bad. Months later I was invited to a party at the apartment of some of my old college buddies. The old, two-bedroom apartment had large rooms, decorated in early-American thrift-store style. Wearing my artificial legs, I dressed in slacks and a short-sleeve shirt, and went to the party.

The mood was festive. When I arrived, I was welcomed by my old friend Ken, who was wearing a huge papier-mâché head, used for cheerleading at college.

"Bob, glad you could make it," Ken said, as he took off the huge head and placed it over mine.

"Hey everybody, do you know who I am?" I asked as each guest entered the dimly lit room.

Later, as I sat on the couch, Kathy, a tall, attractive brown-haired girl I had dated in high school, breezed in. She had been away at college. Immediately Kathy sat down next to me, and as soon as she recognized who I was, she hugged me. "Welcome home, stranger. Good to see you."

"You too," I countered.

"You look great," she said. "You haven't changed a bit." She talked a mile a minute, bringing me up to date on what had been happening in her life. Running out of breath, she finally asked, "What about you? What are you up to?"

"Well, I've been in Nam."

"Yeah, I heard," she said.

"I'm lifting weights back at LaCrosse, working toward my degree. I plan to be a PE teacher or coach."

"That's great," she said. "How'd you like to dance?" and she quickly tugged, trying to pull me up toward the dance floor.

"Didn't you hear?" I said, somewhat startled.

"Hear what?"

"I lost my legs in Nam!"

Did she do a double take! I knocked on my artificial legs, so she could hear that unmistakable hollow sound. "I didn't know, Bob. I don't know what to say. I'm so sorry." But she quickly recovered and said, "As far as I'm concerned, you're still the same guy I knew at LaCrosse."

She got me up anyway, and we danced. On artificial legs I was not a contest winner, but Kathy remarked that I hadn't lost my sense of rhythm.

We dated a few times after that. I told her I was planning to move to California; and she promised to visit, since she had relatives out there. As much as I enjoyed dating during those months, I knew I wasn't ready for a serious relationship.

I began to resume what I considered a normal life, yet part of "my life" was missing. The peace I had once had never returned, and I searched a lot of avenues to find it or something like it. At the time I didn't know what was missing or what I was looking for.

I was working out as often as I could. The amount of weight I could lift increased steadily, as did my body weight. Mom's cooking was hard to resist, and somehow she got the idea that the more flesh I put on my bones, the more power and strength I'd have. I found no real satisfaction in eating, but I continued eating more, hoping to find the strength and maybe the inner satisfaction that had seemed to elude me.

That first winter, drinking beer in a Milwaukee roadhouse, I ran into Wally Karthausser, my five-foot-four sandy-haired buddy from high school. Actually, he was a former rival.

"Hey, Bob," he greeted me, "what's happenin'?" I explained how hard I was working out. "Yeh, man, I'm working out too. Why don't we hang out together?"

"Sounds good to me," I replied. "Let's do it." And we did.

As my weight increased, so did my shirt size. Clothing became difficult to find, especially 4X-Large shirts.

One Saturday Wally and I drove from shopping center to shopping center, searching for a shirt. We found nothing that would fit, and finally Wally offered to go into a big and tall men's shop and inquire while I waited in the car.

When Wally returned he was smiling. The salesman had laughed when Wally had asked for a 4X-Large shirt. "Why son," the clerk said, "don't you have an overrated opinion of yourself? You probably wear a medium in the boy's department!"

Wally helped me get ready for the Wisconsin State Championships in March 1970. I'd heard about them from a physical therapist at the hospital. One of the categories was weight lifting. I started intense training so that by March I was raring to go.

I'd never seen so many wheelchairs in my life as at those Championships, and all filled with athletes eager to compete, eager to show what they could do. Many of these wheelchair athletes had been injured at birth or in work-related or car accidents. I watched race after race, waiting for the weight-lifting contest to be called. Weighing in at 163 pounds, I gave it my best shot and lifted 310 pounds—a clean lift. Then I waited hours more to hear the results. When I heard that name— Wieland—I shouted with delight. There's something wonderful about being the best in any class.

But as I flew home, I knew that that would be my first and last wheelchair contest. The challenge didn't seem great enough. I wanted to compete against able-bodied athletes and see how I measured up against them. In my mind, I was still an able-bodied athlete.

Wally and I continued to hang out together and to work out every chance we got. It was an opportunity for Wally to see firsthand how society treats the disabled. As I wheeled my chair down the street, some people would look the other way;

some would try to help me; some would cross the street to avoid dealing with me.

One day Wally mentioned that many of my friends referred to me as "handicapped."

"Well," I said loudly, fighting back some deep-rooted anger, "I'm not. I'm not a handicapped veteran. I'm a disabled veteran. That's why they call the organization Disabled American Veterans. *Disability*, according to Webster, is the loss of use of a limb or limbs. That completely describes it. I lost two limbs. It's nothing spectacular, that's just how you define *disability*."

"I understand," Wally said, and I knew he did.

I wasn't angry at him, yet I continued my discourse, "Disabled people can fall into a trap."

"What do you mean?" Wally wanted to know.

"Well, the trap of not working to be as self-reliant as possible. When a disabled person relies on others more than he or she has to, that person has less of a chance for the total development of body, soul, and spirit. I know that some people need assistance, and that's different. But I don't consider the loss of my limbs a serious injury. Even those who suffer serious injury should still be encouraged to do everything within their means and have every opportunity to express themselves and make a contribution to society."

By this time I had Wally's attention. Maybe to get me riled up even more he reminded me of a mutual acquaintance who had told me that I'd do much better if I'd only act more disabled, that I would get more attention and help that way. "For the last ten years or so the slogan 'Help the Handicapped' has influenced society's thinking. As long as that mindset is projected, non-disabled people will be convinced that the handicapped need special help. They've heard it on the radio and TV—that you *have to help* the handicapped."

Wally cut in. "So society has helped convince disabled people that they're handicapped and that they need help?"

"Right, and so they've lost their independence and sense of self-worth. They see themselves and are seen by others as inferior. Recently I read a statement: 'God doesn't make junk.' How could he? We're made in His image."

It was good for me to hang out with Wally; he listened to me, understood me, and accepted me as I was.

That year at home passed quickly. Soon it was winter again. The day the first snow fell, I started packing. My dad walked into the bedroom and looked around at my opened closet and bureau drawers. Somewhat bewildered, he said, "Where are you going?"

"California." Had he forgotten that this was part of my plan?

"You mean the *State* of California?"

"Yeh, California."

"That's located someplace out west?"

"That's right," I said as I packed. By now the flurries had turned into a steady snowfall.

"Can I help you pack?" he asked.

"Yeh, that'd be fine."

My mom soon joined us, asking the same questions, not quite believing what she was seeing, "Are you really going to California?"

"Yes, Mom, I am."

"Bob, are you sure that's what you want to do? California's so far away."

"Yes, Mom, I'll be all right. Things will be easier for me there than here. I really can take care of myself."

So, together, the three of us packed my yellow-and-black Cadillac Eldorado. The back seat looked like a sporting goods store, crammed with weights, lifting bench, and artificial legs. I hugged my parents and thanked them. Then I looked the other way so Mom would think I hadn't seen her tears. As I started the car, I promised to write and to call once a month.

"Don't worry, Mom," I said with my eyes if not my lips. "Remember—I'm a survivor."

5

CALIFORNIA, HERE I COME

Like thousands before me, I drove west full of hope for a new life.

The trip went smoothly. I was in awe of how beautiful America is, and that awe planted a seed: Maybe someday I'd have time to see more of the country firsthand—after college, of course.

When I arrived in Los Angeles in the fall of 1972, I enrolled in six classes at Cal State, L.A., including fundamentals of baseball, basketball theory, and beginning wrestling.

After surveying the landscape, I moved into the Oakwood Garden apartments. My dog, Zeus, and I ate porterhouse steaks and hamburgers that I bought at the commissary at Long Beach. Zeus especially loved hamburger and ate enough for both of us—until he mysteriously disappeared after a year, and I had to eat hamburgers alone.

I was grateful for having adjusted to life in a wheelchair—maneuvering up, down, through, or around curbs, ramps, doorways, steps, sand, gravel, slush, and water. Here in California everything was so spread out and every place you needed to be was so far away from where you were. At first I was late for everything, until I learned that I needed to allow

myself plenty of extra time. I'd tell my friends I wasn't running
by the same clock as they were.

Soon after I began classes I met a vet named Isaac Ruiz in
the counseling offices at Cal State. I saw a swarthy-looking,
dark-haired guy sitting behind a desk, counseling someone. He
looked more like a character actor than a counselor. When he
spoke, he waved his arms like a traffic cop at rush hour.

As I watched, I noticed a few people behind me in the line
had declared their own rush hour. They'd pushed ahead of
me. Not being one for patience, I shouted, "Hey, what does a
guy have to do to get waited on around here?"

Five-foot-ten Isaac, who was a little impulsive himself, even
hot-headed, nearly jumped over the partition. "Are you too
good to wait your turn? What are you, a special case or
something?"

"Hey, man," I said, "I've been waiting my turn, and I've got
better things to do than sit around here all day."

Just to prove his point, Isaac made me wait twenty more
minutes before he helped me.

That was the beginning of a great friendship. We discovered
that we had a lot in common, and soon I wasn't eating
hamburgers alone anymore—but with Isaac.

One day at lunch Isaac asked me how my social life was
going. Half kidding, I said, "Oh, yeh, the California co-eds'
ideal man is a strong, athletic, white, double amputee! Out of a
thousand women, even ten million, how many would say, 'My
number one choice for a mate is a double amputee'? And
besides, Isaac, I'm particular about whom I date."

Being into physical fitness, I was looking for a woman who
was also fit. I knew that even the kindest, most successful
woman wouldn't interest me if she wasn't in good shape. "I'm
not in any hurry, Isaac. My wife is going to be physically fit."

Part of my class requirement was to teach two days a week at
L.A.'s Whitney School for disabled students—of all sizes,
shapes, colors, and disabilities. It was one of the greatest
teaching experiences of my life. The school, at Western and
Adams, was about twenty years old; the building had long
hallways and a working gymnasium.

The students felt comfortable with one another and got along well. Those who could function a little better than the others knowingly or unknowingly challenged their peers. Even the kids who couldn't talk well would try to so hard to express themselves and encourage their friends.

Most of the twenty-five students were mentally slow. The first day I told the students that being involved was the most important part of this class, that everyone would have a certain responsibility. But I gave them a number of options and suggested they accept the responsibility they felt most comfortable with.

Even though I'd been warned ahead of time that sometimes the kids challenged somebody new, I didn't have any problems. From the first day, I let them know who was in charge. Kids respect strength. And more importantly, I showed I was concerned about them. As I cared about them and shared my love with them, they quickly realized I wanted them to succeed. They had all the ingredients of the perfect class.

I taught them all the basics that can be learned through repetition. I showed them that a number of things have to take place to develop muscular strength. First, in working out with weights, you have to increase the number of repetitions and/or the poundage gradually. Second, you have to decrease the amount of rest time between sets. Third, you have to increase the number of workouts per week and then increase the period of time you hold a given position.

To support one another, the class split into groups of four to work as weight-lifting teams. One guy lifted. Two guys loaded the bar. One guy spotted, and they rotated positions.

I talked to them about full-range motion, complete flexion, and complete extension. I taught them exercises for the ten major muscle groups: the chest, back, triceps, biceps, shoulders, forearms, quadriceps, hamstrings, calves, and abdominals. I emphasized that each muscle group had to be thoroughly exercised. For example, for the chest we did a bench press, using a different weight for each individual. One guy, who may have weighed two hundred pounds and already had some training, pressed more than a hundred-pound freshman, who could lift only the empty bar.

For the back muscles we did dead lifts, and to exercise the shoulders we did military presses. We did parallel-bar dips for the triceps and curls for the biceps. To exercise the abdominals, we did half or quarter sit-ups with our knees bent. Working the quadriceps, we did squats. For the hamstrings we did leg curls; for the calves we did calf raises, and we did the reverse curl for the forearms.

I explained why it was important to rest between sessions, to allow the muscle fibers to recuperate, and I went through some general training programs for endurance, maintenance, and power.

I also taught the students the basics of nutrition—whole grains, fresh fruits, fresh vegetables, nonfat dairy products, and limited amounts of poultry and fish.

Another day at lunch Isaac asked, "What improvements have you noticed?"

My report was enthusiastic: "The kids' self-esteem has improved; their confidence is great. Their whole outlook on life has changed."

I also spoke to Dr. Jan Seaman from Cal State, L.A., who specializes in physical education for students with special needs. She was impressed with the progress I had made with the students. As a result of my pilot program, Dr. Seaman expanded the disabled program and the adaptive PE program at Cal State.

By the end of the eight weeks, these kids who were physically and mentally disabled could have taught the college students a thing or two about fitness.

One student stands out in my mind: James Johnson. He must have been eighteen or nineteen, a senior in high school. Though epileptic, he was probably the strongest black kid there. James was about six feet tall and weighed maybe one hundred and eighty-five pounds. A good-sized young man, James fell in love with the class; he was always the first one there and the last to leave. I took an interest in James and spent a little extra time with him because I knew he was interested in improving himself and growing stronger.

One day after lifting weights, he grew so excited that he had a seizure. My Army medic training came in handy, and I was able to keep him calm until a nurse arrived. It seems he had forgotten to take his medication. I stayed with him until he came to. I cradled his head in my lap and gently admonished him, "James, you had us concerned for a while. Hey, man, you could have hit your head and really messed up the floor with your blood." He smiled weakly. "James," I said, suddenly very serious, "promise me you'll take your medication, okay?"

"Yeh, man, I'll do it for you."

"No, you've got to do it for *you*."

Over and over I'd tell the students three important words: "Strive for success." I let them know that it wasn't important that their success be acknowledged, because what was successful to one person may not be successful to another. At first some students at the school couldn't do even one sit-up. In a matter of ten weeks all the kids had done at least one sit-up. You know, ten sit ups isn't that significant—unless you look at it in relation to the starting point. It was the effort they put into it. That made their progress outstanding. Each kid received an A.

I enjoyed the class and was sad to see my assignment end. I suspect some of them will never forget that year—I know I won't.

Soon after my assignment at Whitney I graduated from Cal State with a degree in physical education. Almost immediately I went to work, teaching PE at my alma mater. I'd reached my first goal—and it felt good.

One day during a break from my classes, I dashed out of the university and wheeled into a nearby fast-food restaurant. More hamburgers. As I rolled in, a beautiful six-foot, golden-skinned woman was walking out. Did I want to catch her attention! "Could I get a hello?" I asked as she passed by and through the door. Well she gave me more than a hello. She came back in and set down with me while I ate. I felt comfortable with her immediately. Her name was Jackey, and as we left, forty-five minutes later, I knew that she was the first woman in California who had accepted me for myself. She was on her way to a modeling interview and I had to get back to school, so we exchanged phone numbers and made arrangements to meet again at a restaurant in Pasadena.

Though I considered this dinner a "date," I didn't take it too seriously; I had been disappointed before. When she showed up promptly at six, as promised, I was pleasantly surprised. Hmm, maybe *she* was taking this seriously. She was dressed in black and wore a great perfume called Opium. She looked as good as she smelled. Dressed up, wearing high heels, Jackey, the model, was "all legs."

That night I discovered that this was one talented woman— an award-winning fashion designer, a model, a dancer, and also a homebody who loved to cook and garden. For fun she raised Saint Bernards. Most of all she was a warm, sweet woman who seemed to like me as much as I liked her. By the end of that first date, I was saying to myself, "Go slow, Bob. Go slow!"

As I went home that night I remembered a wrestling match at school. I'd trained so well that my upper body strength had tripled, and after some maneuvering, I had pinned my partner, Jerry Lawrence, to the mat. Things had gotten a little out of hand and by the time he'd left he was black and blue with bruises. "Imagine being beaten by a guy with no legs," Jerry had laughed. "What will my girl say?"

That last line had stuck with me. "What will my girl say?" Jackey was the first woman I'd met in a long time whose opinion mattered to me. You might say she was on my mind— a lot.

One of my next dates with Jackey almost ended in total disaster. We were at an amusement park called Magic Mountain, having a great time. Without thinking we piled into seats of one of those upside-down rides. I nearly fell out!

I spent more and more time with Jackey. As we were seen in public, friends and associates commented about our relationship. We were from two different worlds. I—a two-foot-ten-and-a-half-inch white athlete from middle America—was an only child, raised by suburban parents. Jackey—a six-foot, glamorous, sophisticated black model and dancer—had six brothers and sisters and had been raised in Texas by her grandparents, with her mother, Marshell, in the background.

With Jackey I could share my inner feelings. During one of our quiet dinners at home, I poured out the frustration I'd had with women when I came home from Vietnam minus two legs. Whether in a relationship or in training, I had always appreciated a direct answer. I could handle someone telling me no, even a woman saying she wouldn't go out with me. But suddenly I was getting long lists of excuses, no straight answers. "So I had to put the clues together and figure it out for myself. Maybe the reason I wasn't able to date attractive women was because I had been injured." Jackey understood.

I don't know why, maybe just to see how she'd respond, I said that I thought I was a reasonably intelligent person. I looked into her dark, soulful eyes to catch her reaction.

"Yes, Robert, you are very intelligent," she assured me in her melodic voice.

The more I spent time with her, the harder I fell.

One night Jackey's mother joined us for dinner at home. She was full of stories I was eager to hear. "Even when she was a little girl, Jackey was sensitive to the needs of others. Why one day after school she walked a new girl home—to the other side of town—because the child was scared and afraid she'd get lost. Then Jackey got lost finding her own way home and didn't show up until it was dark. Were we worried!"

Who knows when friendship between a man and a woman turns into love? For me, at that stage in my life, love had given me license to set up housekeeping with Jackey. Wasn't that the modern way? I couldn't tell you exactly when I first knew I was in love, though I do remember the day I realized I never wanted to lose her.

I had even started to take Jackey's companionship for granted a little—until one evening she didn't call as she'd promised. Concerned that something had happened, that she was hurt or in trouble, I began calling everyone we knew. No one had seen her or heard from her. For the first time in my life, I knew what it was like to be overtaken by jealousy. I began to imagine what she might be doing. After all, she hadn't called, and it was now early morning. Where was she? So jealous and angry did I become—due to my own imagination—that I was like a man possessed as I went to her closet, burned her clothes, and then left the ashes by the front door. What was wrong? I wondered, and the question grew to gigantic proportions.

Just as I was getting ready to go out to look for her, she walked in. I exploded in anger. "Don't mess around with my emotions!" I warned, which, of course, was my immature way of saying, "Please . . . I love you . . . don't hurt me."

Jackey had been tied up in some record negotiation. Several times she had tried to call me, but the line was busy because I was calling everyone I knew to find her. We bantered back and forth awhile. At first she couldn't believe that I would actually burn her clothes, and she became very upset. I felt terrible and did all I could to make it up to her. Later I replaced all her clothing and more. And later still, we both laughed about the whole affair.

After our make-up hug, I knew I never wanted to lose this woman. For the first time ever, I was in love.

Not long after, Jackey's show business dream began to come true. Just as I encouraged her in her dream, she encouraged me in mine. I wanted to compete in weight-lifting contests against able-bodied men.

I set my sights on the United States Powerlifting Championships in August of 1977 in Santa Monica. The meet was several years away, but I knew it would be worth the intensive training. I worked out at Vince Gironda's gym in the Valley. The first day I walked in wearing my artificial legs, Vince didn't notice. He just said, "You can dress in the back room." You should have seen his face when I came out in my wheelchair. Look man, no legs!

At that time, my training routine kept me busy, and my life seemed to be going along at a steady pace until one Sunday when I felt drawn to a church that Rickey Tedford had told me about: the Crenshaw Christian Center on Vermont Avenue in Los Angeles. The moment I walked in, I felt the presence of the Holy Spirit. The peace that I had experienced only fleetingly before seemed to reside in that place. I knew I'd found what I'd lost—my deep inner connection with God. Like a rushing river, joy flooded my being.

The pastor, Fred Price, had some strong words on the subject of marriage and commitment. "A real Christian man makes a commitment, then marries the woman of his choice. She wears his ring. He doesn't expect free sex. There is no such thing as free sex!"

I knew he was right, and I knew my relationship with Jackey was wrong. But the risk! Would I lose her if I told her we shouldn't sleep together? I left that church service torn between two emotions: the God of peace asking for my commitment to His laws and my fear of losing Jackey. Yet the contest was one-sided. I repented of my sins and asked God for forgiveness.

When I got home I sat Jackey down for a heavy talk. Jackey understood my feelings and quickly agreed that we would take separate bedrooms until we made more decisions about our future together.

For me the big decision—to marry—was made a lot easier when Jackey herself became a Christian the next August. I rejoiced because I knew we could now establish a truly lasting relationship.

Jackey and I proposed to each other in our living room, and we started to plan a wedding at the Christian University Church in Houston, Texas.

As excited as I was about marriage, I almost didn't make it to the ceremony. Exhausted by the trip from California, I fell asleep watching a televised football game. My brother-in-law Jack woke me up just in time.

Jackey designed her own pink gown, and I was decked out in a beige suit and sported a full beard. My only disappointment was that my parents weren't able to be there to see us pronounced husband and wife.

Because I had to get back to work, our honeymoon became an IOU. Later, we said, when we've achieved some of our dreams and when we have more time—and money.

6

MARRIED LIFE

Jackey and I settled into our two-bedroom house in north San Gabriel, which we shared with our huge, lumbering white-and-rust-colored Saint Bernard, Colonel, and our mixed terrier, Pee Wee. We laughingly referred to Pee Wee as our attack terrier because part of his evening routine was to attack Colonel ferociously, barking as loud as he could. Colonel would just roll over and ignore him—at least most of the time.

One night, Colonel got fed up. He seemed to be asleep when Pee Wee attacked. Colonel quietly rolled over, put Pee Wee's head into his mouth, and held the small dog there for a few moments. Colonel didn't want to hurt Pee Wee. He just wanted to make a statement. We thought maybe Pee Wee had been cured, but, no, the next night he was at it again.

Colonel was the best watchdog I've ever seen. Not mean, just protective. Most people think St. Bernards are cute, but I constantly had to tell them, "Don't mess with this dog."

For instance, one time when Rich, a workout partner of mine, came to the back gate, I said, "Rich, I'll meet you around the front." But Rich, curious to see this infamous dog, reached over the gate and opened it. As soon as I looked out the back window and saw what was happening, I yelled, "Get out of there!" The commotion woke up Colonel, and in a couple of seconds, Colonel had pounced on him. That was the last time Rich ever went in the back yard. In fact, that's the last time we saw Rich for quite awhile.

In the early days of our marriage, I had plenty of time to spend with Jackey. My teaching load at the university wasn't heavy. Once or twice a week I spoke at high school "Strive for Success" assemblies, but they weren't all that time-consuming. We often enjoyed gourmet restaurants, and she was always dressed for the occasion. I'd call her "legs" when she wore high heels. Jackey always seemed to be surrounded by a cloud of perfume, which I loved to buy for her—along with bouquets of roses and jewelry.

Though we spent a lot of time together, I soon learned that Jackey was also very independent. Some men smother their wives; I don't. I respect her wishes when she wants to go window shopping or out with her friends to the movies. Anyway, she likes thriller movies, and I'm not a bit interested. But despite our independence, we keep our romance alive.

Soon, however, both Jackey and I grew busier—Jackey, with her career, redecorating our house, landscaping our front yard, watching over her mother who lived in a guest house on our property, and babying our pets.

I had chores of my own. One day when I was out mowing the lawn a neighbor yelled over and said, "You shouldn't be doing that."

I answered, "Tell that to my wife. She said if I didn't cut the lawn I'd be in a whole lot of trouble!"

We also had our share of disagreements. Normally, Jackey picked up after me, but sometimes she'd lose patience and have to get a little vocal. I would try her patience by arriving home late for dinner. I still hadn't mastered the California freeways. The more I rushed to get places on time, the later I seemed to arrive. I knew—and so did Jackey—that I'd have to make more of an effort to be punctual.

Jackey's brothers and sisters often came over for meals and family get-togethers. My brothers-in-law and I enjoyed watching football, while the women congregated in the living room for "women talk." Those were special times, because Jackey's mother and I were able to grow very close. I appreciated the fact that she and her family accepted me completely, as if they were color blind.

Nor did Jackey ever treat me as if I were disabled. For instance, we loved to go dancing at night spots in Pasadena or at the Whiskey A-Go-Go. Of course, we always attracted attention—since Jackey was a professional dancer. Still, I learned to do a pretty mean boogie standing up in my wheelchair. One evening, a handsome black man tried to cut in. After we explained that we were together, he realized he wasn't going to get a dance from Jackey. Still, as he walked away, I could see him shaking his head.

I kept going to Crenshaw Christian Center, and Jackey went with me when her schedule allowed. Pastor Fred Price was an excellent teacher, and as I studied the Word in the early morning hours, I began to notice some subtle changes in my behavior. The comfort and satisfaction I had been searching for all my life were growing within me. A powerful anointing of the Holy Spirit was daily descending on my life and athletic career.

Even my relationship with my wife took on new meaning. Sometimes couples take each other for granted. The opposite was happening with us. The more I opened up to God, the more I appreciated my wife.

Since preparation was still a key word for me, I was also spending more time in training. I had some of my own fitness equipment, including a weight-lifting machine and about a thousand pounds of Olympic weights and dumbbells. I was still aiming for the United States Powerlifting Championships. Jackey encouraged me to keep on training no matter how busy she was.

Just like my students the year before, I was now working on all of my ten different muscle groups. My routines have always been pretty basic. What was important was not so much the exercises, but the intensity that I created by decreasing the rest period between sets. With that, I'd work to gradually increase the weight I could lift and increase the amount of time I could hold a given position. I could see that as long as I incorporated those principles in my workouts on a daily basis I would continue to make progress.

Every workout, I'd work on one or more muscle groups—arms; back; parallel-bar dips for the triceps; drag down barbell curls for the biceps; reverse curls for the forearms; a barbell seated press for shoulders; curl-ups for the abdomen; pull-ups behind the neck for the back. Some days I'd do better than others, but I kept a careful record of my progress and rejoiced no matter what.

The weight I lifted depended on how many repetitions I wanted to do. With lighter weights I usually did three sets of eight to twelve repetitions. In a bench press I did between 175 and 300 pounds. I'd do three sets of ten pull ups behind the neck pull ups with a wrist grip and curls, probably three sets of eight with sixty to eighty pounds. I did two or three sets of eight dips, with my body weight plus a hundred to a hundred and fifty pounds around my waist.

Vince Gironda, a leader for many years in the field of body building, spent a lot of time with me. He was a wonderful source of motivation. A great teacher, Vince set high standards for the people he worked with, and in terms of perseverance, he would take you as far as you wanted to go. He taught me a lot of the exercises.

In preparation for the United States Powerlifting Championships, I competed in and won a number of weight-lifting meets sponsored by the Police Athletic League. The victories encouraged me. I had a feeling I was going to win the United States Powerlifting Championships' bantam-weight title. I knew that I was up against strong competition, but I was ready—and well prepared.

On the day of the meet, the roar of the crowd was music to my ears. Isaac was there to cheer me on, and Jackey was yelling from the bleachers. Under Vince's training I'd made the weight class. At 122 pounds, I centered in, gave it everything I had, and lifted 303 pounds. That lift was beyond even my imagination—it was a new world record. All the months of discipline, hard work, and striving had paid off. And for a moment, winning tasted so sweet!

But I wasn't able to savor my success for long. Within a few minutes, a group of judges was standing over me and pointing to a rule book. One paragraph near the end of the book stated, "Contestants must be wearing shoes." Otherwise, they were disqualified.

I looked down at the floor and said to them, "Wouldn't you know? Today would be the day I forgot to wear my shoes!" The judges were serious about my infraction and insisted that I didn't have the record—or a title.

My initial reaction was disbelief. Surely some higher official could overturn this ruling. The story couldn't possibly be over. Still, I knew that I'd met my own goal, and that was the important thing. That's what I'd always told my students at Whitney and now real-life was showing me how true it was. Right there on the gym floor I was able to reach out a hand to that judge and say, "That's okay; the joy is in the journey." I had proved that I was a world-class athlete, and no human judge could take that away from me.

As I left the auditorium, I said to myself, *I know that God never closes a door without opening a better one.* If He had closed this door, it was okay. I would just keep my eyes open for the next—and better—open door.

I spent more time than ever reading my Bible, attending Crenshaw Christian Center, which had moved to Los Angeles, and listening to Pastor Price. I was finding out how God works in our lives—very simply. As I began speaking to high school groups, I soon discovered that many people are looking for just the opposite—complex answers.

The more I studied the Bible, the more hungry I grew for the Word of God. I realized we are spiritual beings first. Our souls, minds, emotions, and bodies are important, but at the core, we are spiritual beings. I concentrated on letting God train the spiritual man within me, allowing the Holy Spirit to operate.

I loved my time alone with God. Jackey was a night person, so while she slept in the early morning hours, I prayed and read passages from Scripture.

My friend Isaac came to church with me, and we studied the Bible together, both in class and at my home.

One day Isaac invited me to watch him audition for the part of Mondo on the television series "Chico and the Man." The room was full of people—actors and agents—but mostly Isaac's family. There were so many there that when the casting director announced that Isaac had been chosen, the cheers and applause sounded as if the Lakers had just won the championship.

I was amazed that I was now friends with a bona fide television actor. When Isaac said, "Hey man, you'll be next," I said, "Who knows? Maybe someday I'll work as a stunt man!"

But at that moment in my life, I only wanted three things: to study the Bible, be a good husband, and compete as an athlete. In a sense, I wanted to train both my body and my spirit. And as I continued my early morning reading of the Bible, I was amazed how its power grew in all aspects of my life.

Taking Pastor Price's advice, I stopped marking up my Bible with yellow highlighters. He said that the Spirit would help me recall Scriptures as I needed them. It worked. I almost felt as if I was in the boot camp of Bible training, getting ready for the big war, a major event that might shake up my entire life.

Because of that feeling, I spent as much time with Jackey as possible. We seemed to be storing up memories, getting ready for our next big challenge. I took her to plays, to movies, on shopping trips. I helped her choose new furniture for our home and made sure she knew how much I appreciated all of her gifts.

All the while, I felt a growing concern for America's kids. A pattern was emerging—a spirit of rebellion, carelessness, bitterness towards parents and authority figures, overwhelming materialism, and apathy. I saw signs of teenage gangs, violence, drug trafficking, steroid abuse, and alcoholism.

Things weren't much better with many of the Vietnam veterans I kept in touch with. Many were still suffering from post-traumatic stress, horrible nightmares, relational problems, and physical and emotional effects of Agent Orange.

I began to realize that there was only one permanent solution for the restless students and the vets. They had a spiritual hunger. They were hungry for the personal touch, fulfillment, and love of Jesus Christ. And how would they find the answer to their problems unless someone told them?

I began to pray much like the prophets of old, "Here am I

Lord, send me!" To my surprise, my schedule began to fill up
with speaking engagements. Perhaps this was the big shake-up
I was expecting. Before long, traveling on weekends became
the rule, not the exception. A new pathway was opening before
me. I could reach kids and help change their views by speaking
at high school assemblies all across the country.

A short time later I called the United States Powerlifting
Championships representative and asked him for an update.
When he asked me to wait a minute and put me on hold, I
hoped for the best. *Good,* I said to myself. *They're going to tell
me my record stands.* I was already thinking about the call I was
going to make to Jackey to share the news, when the rep got
back on the line: I'd been banned from competition forever!

Suddenly that phone seemed as heavy as a barbell. It seemed
as if the closed door had slammed in my face. And yet—I had
a peace about the entire situation. My years of dedication *had*
been for a purpose, because God was—and always is—in
control.

One day, many months after that phone call, I was watching
ABC's "Wide World of Sports." They featured an extraordinary
Canadian man, Terry Fox. Terry had lost a leg from cancer,
yet he was valiantly walking across Canada. I was impressed.
What Terry Fox was doing just didn't happen overnight. He
prepared. He worked out. He fell down and picked himself
back up. But Terry was meeting his goal by perseverance. He
was well on his way across the country and he was raising
money for cancer research. I told Jackey about Terry.

One door had closed, it was true. But another would open
soon. And again I prayed, "Here I am Lord, send me."

7

A DREAM IS BORN

The next week I had a meeting with Dennis Estabrook, a five-foot-nine, dark-haired triathlete in his early thirties. When he found out I had been banned from weight-lifting competition, he said, "Why don't you enter a triathlon."

"I'll think about it," I said.

A few weeks later I met with Harry Sneider, a celebrity-athlete trainer at Ambassador College in Pasadena. Sneider was about five-foot ten with silver hair and blue eyes. After Cal State, where I had trained on an old-fashioned, dusty, dirt track, this facility was an impressive sight. Immaculately clean, it looked almost too perfect to be real.

Running on the track was body builder and Mr. Universe Mike Menser; Dwight Stone, the world-record holder in the high jump; and James Butts, the silver medalist in the triple jump. Harry was coaching some of these athletes for the 1984 Olympics.

As I watched, Harry said to me, "Can you imagine your lap time if you still had legs?" Then a light bulb seemed to go on in his head. "Wait a minute, Bob. You're a champion! Let's give you something to strive for." His philosophy was similar to mine. "Anytime a disabled person is denied something, something equal or greater will occur if he turns to God, makes a plan of action, and acts on it. The beauty of it is that God gives answers to people who turn to Him." Then with a twinkle in his eye, Harry asked me, "Have you ever tried walking on your hands and your stumps?"

Harry challenged, "I wonder what you could do a lap in—on your arms? Just one lap—296 yards."

I said, "I don't know, Harry. I just don't know how fast I could do it."

Harry kept talking. "Why don't you get out of that chair, and let's give it a shot. You've got nothing to lose and everything to gain."

Nothing to lose! I climbed out of the wheelchair and swung my body toward that track. I walked bare-handed around the first curve. At first flat-handed and then on my fists, I could see and feel the bruises, then the blisters. Despite the pain and the hot sun, I was determined to finish the lap. And I did—nine minutes and forty-eight seconds later.

"Hey," he said, looking at his stopwatch, "I knew you could do it. I knew you could!"

The exhilaration that flowed through me at that moment was one of the most intense feelings I've ever felt. I knew we were onto something big.

"Bob," said Harry, "what could you do a mile in?"

I just smiled.

As I left the track that day, Harry said, "Come back tomorrow, meet me here at 6:00 A.M."

And I did. Day after day I walked laps around the track. A lot of people watched. From the looks on their faces I knew they thought I was crazy. Some of the athletes said, "This is circus stuff! Why doesn't Bob just stay in the wheelchair? It looks undignified." But other people cheered me on and thought it was a great idea.

Right at the start, Harry asked, "Bob, what do you think of all this?"

I replied, "My concern is to please God, and I feel He has blessed this idea."

Some days Harry and I would get talking about America and the way it was built—on great pioneering spirit. In one of these conversations Harry remarked, "This nation was built by creative and positive people who had tremendous setbacks. Look at all the great men. They had tremendous obstacles to overcome in their lives. I feel you're going to inspire millions of people, Bob. That same pioneering spirit is in you. You're like those men who struck out through the forests and over the rocks and overcame the difficulties. If you walked even ten miles on your hands, you're in the same league as those guys."

At that moment the "Spirit of America" slogan came to me during prayer, and I accepted it. Harry's challenge caught fire. As I left that day, he said, "I feel you have a chance to pioneer something great for many people. Let's start training with that in mind." Before long I was walking up to four miles at a time, wearing a twenty-six-pound weighted vest and size-one running shoes on my hands.

Harry's first thoughts were for me to try something small, like a walk from Pasadena to San Francisco, or maybe from Pasadena to Phoenix.

But God was mapping out in my mind a bigger project. I remembered Canadian Terry Fox's walk, and the Lord was giving me a new twist. I said to Harry, "I want to walk all the way across the country and share my testimony. We could use it as a fund-raising event, encouraging corporations and individuals to pledge money to charity and relief organizations—you know, so many dollars for each mile walked. While in Vietnam, I had wanted to feed hungry kids who were begging for food. Now since I've been back home, I've seen that people here are starving spiritually. I want to introduce them to Jesus. I want to do anything I can to stop both physical and spiritual hunger."

Harry thought for a minute. Then he looked at me with a smile and said, "Go for it!"

When I mentioned the idea to Jackey, she looked at me for a long time without saying a word. "I may be gone for as long as a year," I explained.

She thought for a few moments. "Well Bob, if you feel that's what God has called you to do, I'll support you. You can count on me."

"What if I can't do it in a year and have to be gone longer?" I asked, just to be on the safe side.

"Go for it," she said. "I'm with you every step of the way."
And I was confident she would be.

I started training immediately—eighteen long months of
hard work. My favorite training location was the ocean beach
because of the outstanding air quality and peaceful atmos-
phere. School was in session during much of that time, which
meant that the beaches were not usually very crowded.

I began training in April 1981, and worked throughout the
summer. As winter approached, the ocean water began to cool
off. And when the sun went down, the temperature dropped
dramatically. On several occasions I experienced the initial
stages of hypothermia. In fact, I almost passed out a couple of
times when I was by myself. One evening I had just enough
strength to make it to the car and open the door. I pulled
myself up, laid down on the seat, and broke into a cold sweat.
When I came to, I was soaking wet. Within a few minutes I felt
I had the strength to start up the car and head home. About a
mile down the road, everything started to spin. I had to pull
over and lie back down. I did this about six times before my
body got back to a regulated state. I scared myself that night.
But I learned to be more careful. I wondered if it was a good
idea to tell Jackey—or Harry—how foolish I'd been.

On another occasion I passed out in front of a whole
auditorium full of students. Carl Karcher had invited me to do
a "Strive for Success" motivational talk for the Servite High
School football team in Orange County.

I had just finished telling the students that I was going to
walk across America. I said, "Now I want to turn the program
over to Mr. Karcher," then I wheeled over to the grass, got out
of the wheelchair, and passed out cold. When I came to, I was
somewhat embarrassed. I knew it appeared to the students I
wouldn't be able to make it across the street, let alone
America. On the other hand I knew—and they didn't—what
my schedule had been like the previous week. I had worked
myself to the point of exhaustion. I asked to lie down for a
while and, when I did, my body quickly recovered. It was
obvious to me—and to Jackey when I told her—that I needed
to pray for more wisdom in learning to pace myself.

My favorite beach spot was near a restaurant called Gladstones for Fish. I'd park my car there and walk about five miles down to the Santa Monica pier, and then back, though I would vary the trip. To be out there by myself, where the beach would end near five hundred yards of rocks, was an exhilarating experience. To rest, I would sit on a rock and watch the waves. Just me, the ocean, and the rocks. I'd play games with the waves, or rather, they would play games with me. I would sit fifteen feet back and think I was perfectly safe. Then a big one would come in and almost wash me away. Before I knew it, I'd be soaked. And a few minutes later, I would walk back in the hot sand, letting the wind blow me dry.

Although my friends loved to predict how far I'd walk on any given day, I never knew my energy level or capacity for a day until I started walking. Many times, far from the car, I wouldn't know if I had enough strength to get back. Sometimes as the beach grew dark, I'd hitchhike along the Pacific Coast Highway, back to Gladstones. I'd sit there along the side of the highway holding my thumb out. I think most drivers were afraid of me. All I had with me was a bottle of bee pollen containing a limited nutritional value. After a while I learned to know my limit.

A reporter called one day and wanted to do a story about my training. I told him he could find me about 3:30 P.M. when I'd be down near Gladstones, heading toward the pier. He explained that he didn't know me or the area, and I replied, "Well, just start heading down toward the Santa Monica pier and ask someone if they have seen the guy with no legs."

After I hung up, I got a couple of urgent calls that delayed me. I knew I'd be late, but I had no way of contacting this reporter. When we finally found each other, he wanted to talk about the unusual reactions when he'd asked sunbathers, "Excuse me, did you see a guy with no legs walking on his arms headed toward the pier?" They thought he had flipped out. He was delighted to see me, only if to prove that I really did exist!

Despite cautions and disbelief, I held onto my dream. Anybody can commit to a dream like mine for a week or two weeks or a month, but for eighteen months I was one hundred percent committed to what I knew I had to do—even when I was faced with additional financial challenges. Because promoters had promised me support, I took a leave of absence. I trusted God to supply my needs one day at a time.

He did. Speaking engagements became more frequent than ever. I looked for corporate sponsorships.

Harry and I still worked out in the weight room regularly. One of my short-term goals at that time was to master the two-finger planche (a push-up with your weight on two fingers and with no feet—or stumps—on the ground). I knew I would eventually get it. I felt that my faith in the supernatural power of God and my willingness to practice finally made the feat possible.

I also walked along Santa Anita Boulevard, which was good because of the incline. It was 2.7 miles on Santa Anita from Foothill Boulevard up to the end of the median and then back down. I always walked uphill first, putting out a lot of energy. Then coming down wasn't so hard. I'd turn around and go up and back again—5.4 miles, total. Of course the challenge there was being so close to such a busy road. The exhaust of some of those city buses going up Santa Anita would just about knock me out. Sometimes I'd take a break from my Santa Anita "run," and slip away to Mayor Don Pellegrino's house. Don and his wife were very helpful and gracious to me during my intensive training period.

As September 1982—zero hour—grew nearer, I was really looking forward to my departure. Some people thought my training had dragged on for too long. People who didn't know me were beginning to think the whole thing was a lark. Back in April 1981 they'd heard that I was going to start this walk and now, eighteen months later, I hadn't even begun.

Others may have doubted, but I never did. I knew that once they said, "Go," I would be home free. I would get to Washington, D.C. Only God or I could stop the process. I knew He and I were in agreement. I felt nothing is impossible with God.

Though Isaac had agreed to travel with me, I felt we needed one more person to drive the motor home, which had been loaned to us. In early September 1982, while speaking at a Full Gospel Business Men's meeting, I met Chuck Damato and mentioned to him our need. "Know anyone you might recommend?" I asked. Two weeks later he suggested that we talk with his twenty-two-year-old son, Tom. After much prayer Tom said, yes, he could commit one year of his life to the journey. It was all set then; Tom and Isaac would walk along with me on the journey for company and to help facilitate our accommodations and schedules.

The night before I was to start, Isaac and I went to Sears to buy me a new pair of jeans. I'd wear them on my first day out and they'd last well into the trip. I had them on the next morning when I said good-bye to Jackey. She had chosen to remain in the background for a number of reasons. The most important was that I wanted to protect her.

With her kisses and assurances and best wishes in my thoughts, I left for Independence Hall at Knotts Berry Farm in Buena Park. Approximately three hundred people had gathered, and I hadn't imagined so many would come to see me off. Assemblyman Mike Antonovich read a proclamation. "On your mark, get ready, get set, go!"

I took my first step of my 2,784.1-mile journey to Washington, D.C.

Even before I'd stepped out of the security of the theme park, I heard a heckler shouting out profanities and threats. My eyes quickly scanned the crowd and I found him. Sitting in the driver's seat of a car, he looked as if he intended to plow me down. For a brief moment I wondered if Satan intended this walk to end before it began. Could it possibly be? But the man was escorted away by police.

I had begun the ultimate challenge of my life.

PART TWO
HIGHLIGHTS OF THE
SPIRIT OF AMERICA WALK

8

CALIFORNIA SUPPORT

What a send-off! Reporters followed Tom, Isaac, and me, and crowds lined the sidewalks to wave their support. Having seen the story in the paper and on the television news, they came out, willing to share what money they could spare so that hungry people could eat. I felt as if I was just one small part of a tremendous team that was working toward a worthwhile goal: feeding the spiritually and physically hungry people of America.

Within a few hours, however, I realized something was wrong. I had slipped up on one important detail. I had trained on sand at the beach and on grass along Santa Anita Boulevard. But my real journey would be along sidewalks and shoulders of roads—cement and asphalt. My size-one Sorbathane running shoes protected my hands, but within miles of the start, my new jeans were torn to shreds and my stumps were scraped and bruised.

My friend and adviser Don Pellegrino got me in touch with Connie Naegle, an ingenious leather designer. I took a break while Connie measured and fitted me, and then worked night and day to make me a set of layered leather chaps to protect my stumps. I was confident that these chaps would smooth the road ahead of me—and they worked perfectly.

Our first destination was the World Vision headquarters in Monrovia, California, our plan being to funnel the money we raised through relief organizations like World Vision and the American Red Cross. The public relations department at World Vision had arranged for me to speak to the staff and the press at two o'clock the next afternoon. Since my own schedule was complicated by various logistical problems, my immediate enemy became the clock. I knew I'd have to walk day and night to keep that appointment.

I could walk a mile in about one-and-a-half hours and averaged three to five miles a day. The cars and trucks zipped by us. Slow but sure, like the tortoise in the fable, I just kept plodding along.

After we'd walked about eight miles, the Santa Ana police stopped us—by this time it was two in the morning. They wanted to know what we were doing walking down the sidewalk and crossing busy intersections in the middle of the night. "Where are you going?" one of the officers asked.

"Washington, D.C.," I replied.

"Sure, pal," he quipped. "And what're you gonna do after that?"

"Well, it's going to take me a while to get there."

Again, he reminded me how dangerous it was to walk the city sidewalks and streets. The interstates were even more dangerous, he continued, with the speeding trucks and drunk drivers whizzing by. From the policeman's point of view, we were playing traffic roulette. He did his best to convince us to go back home.

"I'm heading east," I said. And we were on our way again.

Tom, Isaac, and I were encouraged by the number of people who came out the next morning to support us as we headed north to Monrovia. We frequently stopped to chat, to plant seeds of witness and encouragement, and to minister to those who needed help. People of every age and ethnic group— Hispanic, Black, Korean, Vietnamese, Japanese, and Chinese—joined us along the streets of Santa Ana. With its rich cultural mix, my adopted state reminded me of the United Nations. California should be given its own statue of liberty, since so many immigrants continue to pour into this, their new homeland.

And I never knew how many homeless people live in the Los Angeles area—not just adults, but families with small children sleeping in barely running old cars. Many of these parents have jobs, but on minimum wage they can't afford the rent and security deposit on a low-priced apartment or duplex. Why? I wondered. What amazed me was that some of these people even contributed money to the "Spirit of America Walk" to feed families less fortunate than themselves.

Later that day, with only minutes to spare, we arrived at World Vision, where we were honored with a ceremony, a small press conference, prayer, and a generous contribution for which the three of us were very thankful. Earlier, when other potential sponsors had backed out, we had turned our financial concerns over to God. Through World Vision, He had supplied our needs for some time to come, and we didn't suspect this second provision would be sent to us within a few days. And so our contributions continued to come in.

A few days later we stopped in Upland near Griswold's Restaurant on Foothill Boulevard. In the restaurant parking lot, I recognized Senior Pastor Jack Hayford of Church on the Way of Van Nuys, who was with some of his family and associates. Pastor Hayford prayed for the safety and success of our trip and he gave Spirit of America a welcomed donation. I later learned he had received a financial gift earlier that day and had prayed to find a worthy place or person to whom he could pass it on. What a divine provision! We thanked him and headed due east, toward Fontana, where God had arranged a different kind of appointment.

In Fontana, a handsome but obviously troubled Hispanic man in his early twenties stopped his car and walked across the street toward us. He wanted to talk. He had heard about our dream, but actually seeing us had touched him deeply. Just twelve hours earlier his four-year-old son had drowned in the bathtub after an epileptic seizure. His own dreams had been shattered, and I could see that he was hungry for the comfort only Jesus can give. We spoke to him, and right there on the sidewalk he accepted Jesus Christ as his Savior.

It never ceased to amaze me how the Holy Spirit seems to put us in the right place at the right time. Another man approached us in San Bernardino. About forty years old and wearing tattered clothes, this black man was weeping and so torn in spirit that he wasn't able to say anything. For ten minutes his sobs told his story. Eager to share God's grace with him, we prayed, shared our story, and waited for him to speak. He simply emptied his pockets and gave us a donation of ten pennies—everything he had. We thanked him and offered him some of our food, which he accepted with a "thank you" before he walked away. My heart ached for that man whose need was so great, yet who was so willing to empty his pockets when he heard of our dream.

It was soon obvious that the nature of our traveling ministry was to plant seeds in people's hearts. As passersby stopped, I had wonderful opportunities to tell them about God, once I felt they might be receptive. But ten minutes later, on my way out of whatever town I happened to be in, I had to trust God to bring these needy people to other feeding stations that would share more. I could only pray for them.

I was still silently praying for a man who gave us ten pennies when Tom yelled, "Hey, Bob, look out! Look out!" Acting on instinct, I rolled away from the road. When I stopped and turned around, I saw a gypsy-type woman recklessly driving an old dilapidated Ford. With the passenger door wide open, she had been speeding down the street heading straight toward me. Even with Tom's warning she barely missed me. "My guardian angel as always is with me," I said, and I thanked God and Tom for their watchful eyes. It was a close call! Maybe it was time to quit for the day.

Palm Springs, with its clean air and swaying palm trees, was an oasis in the desert. We stayed in our motor home in town in the evenings and walked the interstate during the days. We were used to people stopping to talk, so I wasn't surprised when a blond woman got out of a car and walked up—very slowly, as if walking were a challenge. The closer she came, the more clearly I could read her face, which looked full of surprise. She introduced herself as Sarah Nichols and said, "Not more than twenty minutes ago, I read your testimony and saw your picture on the cover of the Full Gospel Businessmen's *Voice* magazine."

Sarah explained that she wanted to write inspirational films and books. "I was just about to sign with a major talent agency to write books and film and television scripts when an accident almost cost me my life. I was in a car waiting for pedestrians at a cross-walk when suddenly a bus hit us from behind. The next thing I knew, I was in the hospital with a permanent brain-stem injury and a loss of hearing in my right ear. Three discs in my neck were badly damaged. The pain has been constant for five years, and my equilibrium has been affected, which has impaired my ability to read, write, speak, and walk."

She added, "So I know what it's like to be called disabled. And after six years, I'm just able to write again and walk normally."

She had been writing a book for a doctor in Palm Springs and had been praying for another assignment when she'd seen my picture on the cover of the Full Gospel Businessmen's magazine. "I felt impressed that the Holy Spirit wanted me to write a book and film about you! At first, I dismissed the idea. But here you are, half an hour later, right here in Palm Springs. When I saw you I thought you were a mirage!"

I was intrigued by her idea, so I suggested we discuss it further at Mayor Don Pellegrino's house in Arcadia in about a week, when I would be back home on a break.

To be honest, that break was more on my mind than books as I left Palm Springs. I was eager to see Jackey and fill her in on the details of my adventure. When I finally reached my goal just outside of town, I pounded a wooden stick into the ground along Interstate 10. That's where I would start from when I returned from my much needed time of rest and relaxation.

That next week I met Sarah Nichols as planned at the mayor's house, where we shared more of our dreams and goals. She had become a Christian at fifteen, also through Campus Crusade for Christ. She had been writing since her twenties and she had experience in video production. Sarah had worked for Walt Disney and written for CBS television. I said I'd pray about her book-and-film idea when the trip was over, and she offered to pray for me during my trip.

Before I knew it, I was back on the road again, heading for the Arizona border.

On a street in Cathedral City, California, I met a very special three-year-old boy.

"Mr. Wieland," his aunt explained, "we read about your walk in the local paper. We knew you were coming through town, so we've been waiting for you for four days."

The boy gave me his allowance—twenty-one pennies. He and the nameless man who had given us ten pennies made me think about the story Jesus told of the widow' mite—though she gave very little, it was all she had. She gets only a paragraph in the gospels of Luke and Mark, and we aren't told her name, but she's a model for us all.

I remember another small gift that meant a great deal to me. On the outskirts of Indio, California, as we passed an auto mechanic's shop, a Vietnam veteran came out, stood near the American flag in the front yard, and saluted us. He held the salute as long as we were in sight. Silently and with grave respect, we saluted back.

On that leg of the trip I looked forward to November 11, 1982, the day I flew to Washington, D.C., to be one of twenty grand marshals at the unveiling of the new Vietnam memorial—the controversial black-marble wall.

The day was blustery cold, but that was somewhat offset by the warm camaraderie felt by us reunited vets. I, like many of the vets I met, was pleased the public was finally paying tribute to the men and women who had died in Vietnam. I rejoiced with Jan Scruggs, who had committed himself to the project and seen his dream completed, his goal achieved.

As "Taps" was played at the end of the ceremony, I looked over the crowd, huddling to keep warm. There was not a dry eye to be seen. The more than fifty-eight thousand names on the wall included Jerome Lubeno's and the names of almost half of the men in my own company. Suddenly, my sense of personal loss seemed overwhelming.

Again I was back on the road, slowly approaching the Arizona border. By early December I knew my one-year projection for the trip was unrealistic. I'd been walking for three months and I wasn't out of California. At this pace, my two-thousand-mile trek could go on forever!

One afternoon Tom overheard two truckers on the CB radio. One named Pete said, "Hey, Joe, d'you see that?"
The other answered, "No, Pete, what?"
"I just saw a dog walking down the freeway in a T-shirt!"
On one rainy day Tom overheard another trucker on the CB. When it rained, I wore an Army-issue, green rain-poncho and hood; and when this trucker saw me, he radioed, "Hey, George! George! Call the TV station. Guess what I just saw!"
Excited, George replied, "Whadja see, Sam?"
"I just saw E.T. walking down the interstate!"
Those moments always gave Tom and Isaac and me a good laugh. They were always there to keep my spirits up—sometimes bantering about the latest sports scores, often talking about the Lord's work in our lives.
One evening Tom told me a little about his early life. I had wondered why he always wore sun glasses even at night. I thought perhaps his eyes had been injured in an accident, but I didn't want to pry.
Isaac was exhausted, as we all were, and decided to turn in. But tonight Tom seemed in the mood to talk. Our conversation centered on our lives as teenagers. When Tom had moved from the east coast to Northridge, California, in 1969, he had experienced a major culture shock. Before he knew it he was drinking beer and wine and smoking pot. "When I couldn't get high enough on pot, my best friend and I turned to LSD," he admitted.
"One night we were driving around on LSD. I knew it wasn't right. I'd grown up in a Christian family, and I knew better. But just then I started having this weird experience—like I thought I could put my feet through the floor."

Not knowing what to say, I simply kept on listening.

"It started raining, which was particularly scary because I knew I was not in control of the car. So I started praying. I remembered my grandfather used to pray, 'I pray angels around you.' Then I asked my friend, 'Don't you feel there's some kind of presence in here?' He admitted he did. Bob, I know there was an angel in the car with us."

"I believe angels are real," I said.

"My friend just wanted to get home fast, and somehow we made it. But within a few months my friend killed himself. Bob, I was living life in the fast lane. I thought I'd never live to be twenty. Drugs and rock-'n'-roll can burn you out."

I said, "I agree."

Since Tom seemed to be getting more tired as we spoke, I suggested we get some sleep. But he wanted to keep talking.

"Well, then I moved in with a girl. I had a job and things seemed okay for a while—until the day I lost my job and my woman at the same time. I was physically exhausted and just wanted peace. I thought about my friend; he was at peace. So I picked up a hunting rifle and some hollow-point shells—shells so powerful you can blow a rabbit to smithereens."

I listened breathlessly.

"So I picked up this rifle, put the barrel in my mouth, and a little voice inside me kept daring me to shoot myself. So I did. The bullet went up through the roof of my mouth, severed an optic nerve, and left over thirty pieces of metal in my brain."

"Did somebody find you?" I asked.

"No, but I was still conscious. I sat there, covered with blood, and realized I was still alive. 'If there's a God,' I said, 'take over! Do something fast!'

"Somehow, I got out to my truck but I couldn't keep the clutch in to shift. I was shivering, and more and more blood kept pouring out. So I thought I'd walk to my parents' home.

"A policeman tried to stop me, thinking I'd been in a fight. He knew me from before and knew I was pretty wild. But I kept on walking. If I could just sleep, I thought; if I could just go to sleep. But if I had, I wouldn't be here now.

"Somehow I got to the front door. My sister opened it and screamed. 'Oh, my God!' she shouted, 'Tom's been hurt.'

Within a few minutes the ambulance arrived. My dad asked the paramedic, 'What are his chances?' 'Not good,' the paramedic replied. 'We had a guy like this last year, and he didn't make it.' I realized later they were talking about my friend.

"Then with great conviction, my dad said, 'We'll pray for him; he'll be all right.'

"In the hospital, I remained conscious until the moment they started to shave my head. The surgeon discovered a blood clot in my brain and removed it. I suffered damage, due to the wound and the exposure of brain cells to oxygen, and things were very foggy for a couple of weeks. But by some miracle I lived. My first desire was to read the Bible—cover to cover. I had learned the hard way that there's no future with drugs."

I sat silently for a moment, not knowing what to say. Then I simply hugged Tom and thanked God that his life had been spared. Perhaps one of the reasons Tom was still alive was to help me achieve the goal that I had been given to reach.

On December 12, when we got to Blythe, at the Arizona border, people again showed support for the pioneering Spirit of America. Actor Robert Stack flew in by small plane to join the Blythe high school band. Mayor Don Pellegrino, Mrs. Bardella Mason, Hal Ezell, Jim Hampton, Larry Ward from Arizona and many other people from southern California came to see us off, crossing into the wild blue yonder. We rejoiced and praised God that we had reached our first goal— Arizona.

9

ARIZONA: THE DESERT EXPERIENCE

"That man is repulsive. It's the most disgusting thing I've ever seen!"

Someone was talking loudly to Tom—about me. Tom sat in shocked silence and let the man rage on. "I'm gonna stop him from making a spectacle of himself. I'm calling the governor and getting him banned from the interstate."

Tom watched for my reaction. I chose to ignore the insults.

But the desert stranger kept talking. This time to me. "Hey, you shouldn't be walking on the interstate—you're disabled. Hey, if I was disabled, I wouldn't be able to walk on the interstate."

A short time after he left, a highway patrolman came by and said that we would have to get a permit to walk the interstate in Arizona. So after a lot of explaining and patience, we were given a permit, and the Arizona desert was ours to cross.

Still, that encounter seemed to be the beginning of a series of attacks against the Spirit of America. Wasn't it in the desert that Satan had waged war on Jesus, trying to divert Him from carrying out the Father's purposes? There in the Arizona desert Satan and his demons did their best to discourage or even stop us from continuing my mission.

Sometimes our own mistakes discouraged us. Usually Tom

or Isaac would drive the motor home right behind me, like running interference in a football game. One time, when Tom was in the driver's seat, he slowly started gaining speed. So did I. "Tom, slow down," I yelled, but he couldn't hear me over the noise of the traffic. I simply couldn't outrun him and didn't roll out of the way fast enough.

My backside got whomped. Boy did Tom wake up! Next thing I knew he was out of the motor home and running toward me. "You all right? You all right?"

Thank God I was—just shaken up, not hurt.

Nor was that all. When we reached Phoenix, the motor home was hit by a truck that ran a red light. (This time Tom was wide awake!) The motor home wasn't badly damaged, but that was the beginning of the end of our motor-home days. When we made a few phone calls to the vehicle's owners, we discovered a major misunderstanding: the motor home hadn't been loaned to us; it had been *rented* to us. We had run up quite a bill, and Isaac and Tom quickly returned our home-on-wheels to California. Now we were faced with the added challenge of finding places to stay.

As spring turned to summer, we were faced with desert heat. One policeman on the interstate remarked, "It's so hot that even the coyotes chasing the rabbits have slowed down to a walk." A couple of times, the thermometer even hit 120 degrees or more—pretty hot for me, who had trained mostly by the ocean, with its cool breezes, and for Tom and Isaac, who were used to the mild weather of southern California. But we kept moving, constantly adjusting our pace and schedule to accommodate the heat.

Like Jesus in the desert, I knew that I had to cling to one thing—God's promises. In my daily prayer time and in the church services we frequently attended I continued to seek the Lord's face. The Lord was there and even in the desert you never had to travel too far to find His people praising Him.

One Hispanic Four Square Church worshiped with a praise band that I called "120 Tamborines." I spoke to that group with Isaac as my interpreter. It seemed to me that it took him twice as long to say something in Spanish as it took me to say it in English. Was he adding a sermon of his own? I wondered.

That experience in the church must have got Isaac to thinking. On one blisteringly hot summer morning, he told me that he believed the Lord had directed him to move his family to Phoenix and become a minister. He felt he should leave immediately. Tom and I prayed with him, hugged him good-bye, and wished him God's best.

While I knew I would miss Isaac's help and companionship, I was grateful that Tom was still with me.

Not long after that, we ran into even more vehicle problems in the desert. One afternoon Tom left his motorcycle outside and walked into a gas station near Pomerene. When we came back out a few minutes later, the cycle was gone, never to be seen again. We were left only with my own car, what I called "a support vehicle." To get a picture of what it looked like, imagine a vehicle held together by prayer, rubber bands, and silly putty.

But Tom and I continued toward Tucson, as the heat beat down relentlessly. The desert seemed like an ocean of sand. Would it ever end? Because I was making such poor mileage, I decided to try to sleep in an air-conditioned room during the day and walk at night. But my internal clock didn't adjust well to that schedule. By nature I'm an early riser. Even so, it seemed that being a "night person" was my only alternative for a while. I started walking early in the evening, and as the air cooled down, I began to pick up speed.

One night, from far behind me I heard a car radio blaring heavy-metal music. The force and sound of it echoed across the stillness of the desert. What—or who—was approaching? I felt an eerie sense of danger, walking with my back to the traffic.

Not wanting to take any chances, I began to edge over to the extreme left of the shoulder. The pickup, loaded with what sounded like intoxicated teenagers, gained on me, and next thing I knew, I was pelted with water balloons, exploding on impact. Thank God the truck didn't hit me. Once I recovered my composure, I managed to say, "Very refreshing!" For an instant, anyway, I was cool.

Outside of Tucson, Tom reminded me that his one-year commitment was up; it was time for him to move on. I understood. He was, after all, a young bachelor with plenty to do, places to go and see. He had unselfishly given a year of his life, without a great salary or any visible reward. I thanked him, and again wished a departing companion God's best.

So now I was on my own. It was an adjustment, but I could do it. Many of my immediate concerns were met by a man who drove alongside me on Interstate 10, near Tucson. He said his name was Fred Ruth, president and owner of Munday Chevrolet in Benson, Arizona. He shook my hand, offered a few words of encouragement, and left. Since this kind of encounter had happened often enough before, I didn't think anything of it, until minutes later when he returned. He said he had a guest cottage where I could sleep. Within days he set up some speaking engagements that provided some much-needed money.

He offered to do what he could to keep my old "support vehicle" on the road, though its days were clearly numbered. Awaking from a sound sleep one night, I heard a noise. At first I thought someone was snoring. But that couldn't be—Tom was gone. I got up to investigate, looked out the window, and discovered that my old Cadillac was tilted, the tires flat. I found some mechanics in Bowie, Arizona, to fix the tires, and then headed home to Jackey. But on my way the fan belt broke; then the hoses exploded. "Lord, please. Just let me get home," I prayed as I drove west. He answered my prayer: As soon as I hit my driveway, the Cadillac's engine froze up. The car died, right there before our eyes. Was I ever grateful to fall into Jackey's waiting arms!

Jackey was still behind me one hundred percent. But we both knew we soon had to make some decisions. Finances were a challenge. Well-meaning sponsors had promised to donate a vehicle, but it never happened. Our situation was this: Would we sell our house and use part of the money to sponsor the trip or would both the private and public sectors see the need to do this project and raise the level of awareness in our country?

When I left Jackey to return to the road, I knew I'd be taking one day at a time. It was the only way to handle my new solitary routine adequately. I also knew that if another traveling companion was part of the plan, the Lord would provide; He always had. Finances were low, but I had learned to get by on very little.

Back on the road in Arizona, Fred Ruth stopped to talk again. This time, he had arranged for me to buy a discounted red Luv pickup, which suited my immediate needs for transportation.

Near the New Mexico border, an older woman stopped and got out of her car. She looked like a bag lady, very fragile and weak, as if she needed food. Nevertheless, she held out a can of chicken noodle soup and said, "Here take this."

I wasn't sure what I should do, so I offered her a can of Franco American spaghetti. She insisted and I insisted. We ended up trading cans along the interstate.

When I told her I was walking to Washington, D.C., she felt obliged to give me some advice. "Listen, sonny, you're going the wrong way; you have to turn around and go in the right direction." There was no question in her mind or in mine. I took out a United States map and showed it to her. "See," I pointed to Washington, D.C., "that's where I'm going."

She ignored me and said, "Sonny, I told you you're going the wrong way. If you don't turn around, you're gonna get lost!" There was no convincing her.

She was only one of the many homeless people that I met, people who live in almost every part of this country. She made me think of a homeless man I'd met when Isaac and Tom were still with me. Early one morning, before I'd started the day's walk, we saw—and heard—a young dark-haired man in his thirties dressed in tattered clothes. He had loudly cursed and complained at the sight of the Spirit of America banner, "Feed the Hungry," which was draped across our motor home.

When Isaac asked him what was wrong, the man pointed to the holes in the soles of his shoes. "Look!" he screamed. "What about me? I don't even have a decent pair of shoes, and I'm hungry too!"

Tom and Isaac motioned for him to come across the street,

so we could share the Word and some food with him. He did so, grumbling all the way—until he saw me in the motor home. When he saw I had no legs, his face had turned red, and he turned his back and left without a word.

I hoped that that man had reached out to God's love that reaches down to every human—even those whom Jesus called "the least of these"—the people society has cast aside.

I remember another Arizona encounter with castaways. Right about dusk one night I saw two teenagers who looked like Mutt and Jeff walking toward me. The boy looked as if he could be a candidate for the Lakers, while his girl friend was less than five feet tall.

As they approached, they started whispering and decided to cross the highway to avoid me, though there was too much traffic whizzing by for them to get across quickly. The closer I got, the more uncomfortable they grew.

"Hey, what's happening?" I said. "Looks like it's going to be a while before you get across."

They just stared at me.

"Hey, man," the boy finally said, "What are you doing out here? Don't you know you could get killed? No one can see you down there."

"I'm walking across America to raise money to feed the hungry. What are you doing out here? Where are you from?"

"Texas," they answered in unison. The girl's voice was so soft I could hardly hear her. "We're thinking about getting married," the guy explained.

They looked as if they were still in junior high. "How old are you?" I asked.

The girl admitted to fifteen; the guy said he was sixteen.

"Well, what do your parents think about this? Do they know you're here?"

"No, we ran away. Hey, you're not going to turn us in, are you?" the guy asked.

"Hey, I don't even know your names. Why would I want to do that anyway? Maybe you had a good reason to run away from home. Did you? But don't you think your parents are concerned?"

The girl piped up, "My dad's dead, and my mom and her

boyfriend don't care. She's too busy partying to even know I'm gone."

"Yeah, my old man's a pusher. My mom's got a job and my brothers and sisters to worry about. I bet they don't even know we're gone," said the guy. "We're heading to California where couples like us can live without any flak. "We'll both get jobs. . . ."

"You have it all figured out, don't you? I've never been a parent myself, but I know I'd be concerned if you were my kids."

Searching for the right words, I said, "Sometimes parents die, like your dad did. I'm sorry he's not there for you. And other times parents fail us." The girl looked away. "But I know I have a heavenly Father who will never leave me or forsake me or fail me."

I felt a spirit of fear in these kids, and it seemed they were getting ready to leave me behind, but I got a last word in. "I also have a great peace and joy and strength knowing that Jesus Christ is my Lord and Savior."

Before I could say another word, they ran past me. I turned and saw the reason: A highway patrolman was stopping to question them. Before I could reach them, the patrolman had them in the car and drove off. At least I had a moment to plant some seeds.

Near the New Mexico border I walked through a rain shower. After the air cleared a little, I saw a full rainbow stretched out across the whole sky. Rainbows! God's sign to Noah: The flood was over. Genesis 9:13–15 tells the story: "I have set my rainbow in the clouds, and it will be the sign of the covenant between me and the earth. Whenever I pass clouds over the earth and the rainbow appears in the clouds, I will remember my covenant between me and you and all living creatures of every kind."

I felt it was a reminder—that all of His promises are true! Was it a sign that I was walking out of my desert trials? I hoped so. I stepped up my pace, breathing in the fresh air that blows in after a cool rain.

10

NEW MEXICO: MEETING MARSHALL

There's one good thing about walking on the interstates—the mile markers! They let you know exactly how far you've traveled. And yet, without Isaac and Tom, the days and the mile markers came and went slowly.

I worked out a routine with my wheelchair to manage the mechanics of the trip alone. At the end of every day's walk I would mark where I had stopped. The next morning I'd drive two to four miles beyond the marker and park my truck. Then I'd get in my wheelchair and ride back to the marker where I'd hide my wheelchair, usually in some bushes. I'd walk east, to the truck, and then drive back to pick up my chair. In one sense it was doing double duty, and it tired me out more than if I'd had a traveling companion with me. But most important, it worked. Every day I placed myself—and my wheelchair and truck—in the Lord's hands for safekeeping.

One scorching hot summer evening I was especially exhausted. As I drove back to pick up my chair, which I hadn't been able to hide very well, I saw a woman carting it off, squeezing it into her car. "Wait a minute. That's my chair!" I yelled, scrambling out of the truck.

"Oh, I'm sorry," she said sheepishly. "I thought someone just went off and left it."

After that, I posted a sign on the chair: "Please don't steal the wheelchair!" and I left a "Walk for Hunger" brochure between the spokes.

New Mexico mile marker number five was right at the Shady Grove Truck Stop. Though it was well after dark, I hadn't intended to stop—until I was attacked by a swarm of mosquitoes. I knew there were mosquitoes in Wisconsin, but in the desert? Why hadn't someone warned me? Zoom! Zoom! Buzz! Buzz! I retaliated with slap! slap! but I was clearly outnumbered. So I retreated to the truck stop.

"Hey, man, what are you doing out here? Don't you know it's dangerous to be out alone at night?" There was a mocking tone in his voice. A guy who looked like a jolly green giant slowly stepped toward me.

Demanding an answer, he asked, "What are you doing out here, boy?"

I felt God protecting me as I replied, "I'm on a search and destroy mission." I headed toward my Luv pickup truck.

The men seemed to back off as one of them said, "See you later, pal." I made it to my truck and took off.

Most nights I slept in my pickup, wishing Jackey were next to me, especially as the nights grew cold, then colder. One night, late in 1983, outside the town of Deming, the temperature got so low that it became a challenge to stay warm.

When I got up early the next morning, I prayed, as usual, for God's hand to protect and provide. I prayed for Jackey and her needs, not forgetting the bigger issues, such as the country, the hungry for whom I was walking, and of course praise. My pockets held only some loose change—all the money I had. I prayed silently, praising God for my supply, which is new every day. I knew that my heavenly Father would supply my needs.

Later, after I had washed up at a nearby service station, a man approached me. He said he was the owner of the station. "Say, aren't you Bob Wieland?" he asked. "I read about you in the paper. Would you have time to speak at the Lion's Club at noon?"

"Yes, I would."

"Hey, that's great," he said, shaking my hand. "By the way, feel free to fill up when you need gas, at any of my stations."

I thanked him for his generosity and also always thanked God for the provisions He sent my way right on time. Never late. The speaking engagement provided some cash and buying gas would not be a problem in that part of New Mexico.

A few days later I spoke again in the Deming area at a Full Gospel Businessmen's luncheon. A friend I'd made in Spokane, Washington, led to this contact with Red and Ann Cannon, a retired couple from Deming, New Mexico.

The plan was for Red and Ann to meet me at a certain mile marker. At dusk I began to look for them. I kept walking as it grew darker and colder.

I had just begun to think they were lost, when they drove up. He was a stocky man in a plaid shirt.

I was grateful to see them for several reasons, not the least of which was that I knew I'd have a warm bed to sleep in for a few nights. But their hospitality went far beyond my expectations. It was like being home.

After we said our good-byes, I had the strangest feeling something good was about to happen. As I walked along Interstate 10, accompanied by a reporter from El Paso, car after car drove by without my notice. But within a few minutes an El Camino stopped. Its silver-haired driver got out. He introduced himself as Marshall Cardiff, an irrigation specialist working for Global Irrigation in Santa Ana, California. This guy had one firm handshake, which seemed to fit with his athletic frame.

He said, "I know who you are. You're the vet I saw on TV the day you began your walk. I remember saying to myself, 'Oh, my, he's really undertaken something here. Man, if he ever makes it, that will be something!' Good to see you're still at it. Praise the Lord!"

"What brings you this way?" I asked.

Marshall had been attending a seminar at New Mexico State University in Las Cruces. He was in transition. He even thought he might like to settle in New Mexico, so he was looking for a home to rent or buy. He was especially attracted to some grape acreage near Deming.

I introduced Marshall to the reporter who was interviewing me. "I just came by to encourage you and have a prayer with you," Marshall said as he was about to leave. His blue eyes smiled when he talked. The three of us joined hands and prayed along the side of the road. I felt the power and the anointing of the Holy Spirit as we prayed. Saying good-bye, I invited Marshall to join me at a Full Gospel Businessmen's breakfast near Las Cruces.

And sure enough, he showed up. The more time I spent with Marshall, the more I liked him. I felt now that there was a reason we had met. He enjoyed ministering and flying!

When I first mentioned that he might want to pray about traveling with me and taking care of my public-relations work and advanced bookings, his reply was, "Oh, no, Bob, I have a good job." So I let the subject drop.

We began to hang out together. He always came to hear me speak. Watching Marshall, it was obvious that he was somebody who had a great gift for talking to people and for helping them. He had a true servant's heart.

A week later a serious-faced Marshall wanted to talk. "Bob," he said, "I've been praying about what you said, and while reading my Bible I turned to Matthew 19:29: 'And everyone who has left houses or brothers or sisters or father or mother or children or fields for my sake will receive a hundred times as much.'" He couldn't help but think this passage was encouraging him to accompany me all the way to Washington. He said, "I didn't dwell on the message too long before I said, 'Lord, for You, I'd go.'"

I was excited, but just to be sure, I told Marshall I'd pray about it before agreeing. The Lord confirmed my prayer.

Marshall moved quickly and gave his irrigation company two weeks' notice, offering to continue as a consultant. The income would help him, but he also didn't want to let them down by leaving abruptly. When Marshall explained the story to his boss, he immediately released Marshall with a month's pay. "Give it all you've got," he said.

Two weeks later, Marshall joined me, just as I was climbing the Organ Mountains, which resemble the pipes of a giant pipe organ. The beauty, peace, and stillness of those mountains seemed to fit the celebratory mood of the day!

Marshall was perfect for the job. Though a landowner and a successful businessman, he was humble and a wonderful companion. His faith was much like mine in that he knew that faith is active, not passive. We knew that God rewards such faith. So together we took the footsteps (or handsteps) necessary to keep my dream alive of walking across America. We knew that our needs would be met by God's sufficient grace working through people all across this country!

Our steps led us to speaking engagements in every possible place, secular as well as Christian settings. For instance, we spoke to some Army men near the White Sands Missile Range, aptly named, as white sands sparkled and glistened with bits of formica in the sunlight.

After the talk, I suggested to Marshall that we keep walking until sunset and pray that we would meet a couple of people who would like to know the Lord. So we walked, occasionally spotting a king-sized jack rabbit hop across the road, as the colorful sunset inspired us. Just as the last rays of the grand sunset played out, a car pulled up. An older couple stepped out and yelled a hearty hello.

"It's a miracle we found you here," the woman said. The couple had been vacationing in California and had come to find me—in the middle of "nowhere" in New Mexico.

That evening they bought me a big steak dinner, after which we agreed to meet the next morning, since they wanted to walk with me. That morning, I began to share my love of the Lord. They listened intently, and it was obvious to them that my commitment had made a difference in my life. Finally, I said, "Is there anything preventing you from receiving the Lord Jesus Christ?"

"No," they answered.

"Would you like to receive Him now?"

"Yes," they replied, and right there by the side of the road we knelt and they repeated after me the sinner's prayer. "Lord Jesus, I need You. Thank You for dying on the cross for my sins. I open the door of my heart and receive You as my Savior and Lord. Thank You for forgiving my sins and giving me

eternal life. Take control of the throne of my life. Make me the
kind of person You want me to be. In Jesus' name, Amen."

The joy and peace I felt was tremendous. What a homecoming celebration! Those new believers were my parents, Bill and
Ida Wieland! We all had tears in our eyes; Jesus Christ was now
the unifying One in our family.

Our good-byes that day were bittersweet. I wished I could
have spent more time, helping them grow in their faith. But we
did agree to meet when Marshall and I reached Washington,
D.C. I thanked God for their salvation and for sending two
hungry souls to us that night, in answer to our prayer.

As we neared the Mescalero Indian Reservation, a man
stopped along the roadway, introduced himself as Apache
Chief Chino, and offered us two keys to his tepee, which
turned out to be two luxurious suites in his tribe's country
club—Inn of the Mountain Gods.

We were traveling Route 70, which went right through the
reservation. On the edge of it, near Ruidosa, Marshall and I
noticed about fifty cows off in a pasture alongside the road.
Those cattle must have had quite a grapevine, for when the
first one saw me, the rest soon came running and followed us
along the fence. Marshall said they were trying to figure out
who I was and what I was doing.

"I think they're hungry and want to be fed," I said. I pointed
out that many of the cows were chewing their cuds. I thought I
was just making casual conversation, but I didn't know
Marshall well enough at that point to know what I'd gotten
myself into. He gave me the first of his many memorable
science lessons.

"Hey, Bob, do you know why they chew their cuds like
that?"

"Just chewing gum in there, don't you think?"

"No, Bob, they're chewing on regurgitated hay and grass.
Let me tell you what happens—how the cows do it. Now a cow
has four stomachs . . . When the cow chews that grass, or hay,
it goes directly into the rumen, the first stomach. There it picks
up moisture and the specific gravity of the chewed grass

increases. When the cow is through eating, she regurgitates
the food, which is now called bulus."

"Bulus who? I don't see any bulls."

"Bob, this is important. Pay attention. That bulus comes
back up into the mouth and is masticated. Different juices mix
with it until it reaches the state where it is directly shunted into
the reticulum, the second stomach.

"Boy, all I can take care of is one stomach," I said.

"There the digestive juices start breaking it down. The
nutrients are being extracted. . . ." And he went on and on.

Finally I said, "Marshall, can you imagine what your breath
would be like if you were a cow?" He paused for a moment.

"Look, Bob, the cows love it. See that contented look on
their faces?"

"Yeah, like having salad with oil and vinegar on it."

"They're still following us. I think they like us, Bob."

"That's great, Marshall."

Someday I'll write a book—*Life with Marshall!*

Marshall loved to sing hymns. His father had been involved
with the Salvation Army, and Marshall knew every hymn
imaginable. In the deep New Mexico canyons, we'd sing
hymns and shout, "Praise the Lord, hallelujah!" just to hear
the echoes. They were awesome, and the beauty of the steep,
jagged rocks took our breath away.

After helping me get my day in gear, Marshall would go off
adventuring. He loved to explore the countryside on his
motorcycle. Since I had to spend my time walking, most local
points of interest passed me by. But once Marshall rejoined
me, I was able to enjoy the country secondhand through his
long and involved reports.

Marshall found New Mexico a land of contrasts—stark
deserts and ice caves, lava flows and snowcapped mountains.
He explored a historic army fort, traveled across sand dunes,
discovered enough rocks to please any rock collector, and
visited the Aztec Ruins National Monument.

Before we left New Mexico, Marshall visited Heron Lake
State Park on Route 95. That night Marshall was exceptionally
excited, almost like a little kid with a new toy. "Bob, I saw a
golden eagle fly overhead, with snowcapped mountains in the

background. No artist could have painted such a beautiful picture. And on the way back, deer were grazing within a few feet of me."

"Sounds like a great day," I said. "I walked five miles, so I had a good day too!" I usually covered between three and five miles a day.

"Terrific," said Marshall. "We should be in the Lone Star State pretty quick."

Yup. Texas here we come!

Bob's leather chaps and hand guards

On the road—one step at a time

Bob at the California/Arizona border

Bob with actor
Robert Stack at the
California/Arizona border

Twenty-six below zero—the coldest day of the trip, in Vinita, Oklahoma

Marshall Cardiff on his 'cycle

Heading east

Bob in his famous
"E.T." poncho

It's a long, long road

May 14, 1986—walking the final mile; Margaret Harvey is on the left, Marshall on the right

The final few hundred yards

The finish line—
how sweet it is!

Bob and his parents, Bill and Ida, at the Vietnam Wall in Washington, D.C.

To Bob Wieland
Congratulations and best wishes,

Ronald Reagan

In the Oval Office with President Ronald Reagan

11

TEXAS: WIDE-OPEN SPACES

May 31, 1984. We entered the wide-open spaces of Texas. Ki, yi-yippie, I! It didn't take long for us to figure out that Texas is a country by itself, a country within the U.S. of A. In my cowboy hat, I told everyone I met that I was a cowboy!

Marshall sang his hymns as we walked through Texas, enjoying the beauty of the scenery. To see the landscape and to hear Marshall sing his heart out gave me a deep sense of peace and joy.

Marshall was extremely well educated. As we walked near one of the large canyons, Marshall said, as if out of nowhere, "Now Bob, what do you think caused these tremendous canyons?"

I replied, "Oh, probably Paul Bunyan and his plow."

"Well, let me explain it to you, Bob. This is a process of diastrophism. That is, the land is wearing away from wind, water, freezing, and thawing. And as water flows down through the canyon, it forms an inner gorge which is called . . ."

"Thanks, Marshall. Who knows? With your geological lessons, I'll be qualified to give a talk on the landscape of the whole nation."

"I wouldn't be a bit surprised," Marshall said, standing taller than ever.

We saw one of those great canyons "up close and personal." When we reached the town of Canyon, we stayed with Dennis and Marilyn Cannon, the son and daughter-in-law of Red and Ann Cannon whom I'd stayed with in New Mexico. With their three children, the place was a little crowded, so Marshall stayed with another family, Mike and Ginger Stevens, who arranged to get Marshall and me tickets to the play *Texas*, in a beautiful outdoor amphitheater down in the Palo Duro Canyon. At the Allens, we enjoyed an excellent barbecue dinner—beef ribs, corn on the cob, and baked potatoes—out under the pine trees and stars. When the Texans cook beef, they cook it right.

After dinner we went to see the play, which was about early life in Texas, the trials and tribulations of the early settlers. It was so colorful, with the horses, the Indians, and desperadoes. The canyon wall was the stage backdrop, and they actually orchestrated a lightning storm, with electric bolts that shot across the canyon wall. With the accompanying thunderclaps, you felt trapped by a real impending rainstorm. What a memorable production, heightened by the natural and beautiful setting.

One sunny morning on the Texas road I spotted a lamb tangled in barbed wire. As I drew close, it started to fight the fence. What a lesson, I thought. If the lamb could only relax and let go . . . I pointed her out to the shepherd. It seemed like a symbol to me of how we are all like lost sheep before we know Jesus. It was a reminder to me of how important it was for me to share my testimony with anyone who would listen, for salvation is the greatest miracle of all; in the instant we accept Jesus as personal Lord and Savior, we go from darkness into eternal light!

Both Marshall and I had many opportunities to share the Good News. We talked to anyone who would listen. We knelt and prayed with scores of people.

I remember one trucker, Jim, who kept driving by us on his regular route. Finally, he made up his mind to stop. We got down to business right away. Marshall asked him if he knew where he'd be if he died that day. He didn't rightly know, he admitted.

"Would you like to have eternal life?"

"Yes," he replied, "I sure would."

We explained that there are two different kinds of life. One is a self-directed life, where the human self (the personality or ego) is in control, while Jesus Christ is on the outside. This person's interests are decided and directed by himself, often resulting in discord and frustration. The other kind of life is the Christ-directed life, where Jesus is given first place and is invited to direct the life of the person who submits his human will to God's will and yields to Jesus Christ. This person is directed by Jesus Christ and as a result is in harmony with God's plan.

I looked at Jim. His face had softened; there was a glimmer of light in his eyes. The three of us knelt together, said the sinner's prayer, then hugged one another. I read Revelation 3:20 aloud: "Here I am! I stand at the door and knock. If anyone hears my voice and opens the door, I will go in and eat with him, and he with me."

I explained to our new brother in Christ that Christ, who was now in his life, would never leave him nor forsake him. By now Jim's entire face had softened; according to 2 Corinthians 5:17, he was a new creature in Christ.

Marshall explained to Jim how important it is to read the Bible daily and study and learn the Word (John 15:7). "Begin with the Gospel of John," Marshall said, "and check out Acts 17:11."

I added, "It's important to find a church home as soon as possible." I explained that I had received Jesus as a young adult through some guys from Campus Crusade for Christ. "But, I didn't follow through when I went to Nam. I tried to control my own life for years, until I heard Pastor Fred Price teach the Word of God and began to meet with other believers at Crenshaw Christian Center. I began to discipline myself to both read the Word and pray."

Jim doubted he could find a church, since he traveled all the time.

"Pray about it," I said. "Ask God to lead you to a church that will serve your needs. Perhaps you can visit different churches along your route, if that's all you can manage."

Jim said that he'd try, and that he'd stay in touch. I gave him our Spirit of America California address and said good-bye.

But not every encounter was a success. Shortly after we met Jim, another trucker stopped, probably out of curiosity. Encouraged by Jim's salvation, Marshall and I did our best to talk to this guy, but he wanted nothing to do with the Good News. He left in a hurry.

Marshall and I ministered in all kinds of churches all across Texas: Roman Catholic, Presbyterian, Methodist, Baptist, Pentecostal, Assemblies of God, plus nondenominational Bible churches. We wondered if these different denominations realized that all that seemed to divide them was form and doctrine. In truth, all Christians are one in the body of Christ. Sometimes, it seemed as if Satan had caused divisions among the Christians over small, legalistic points of contention.

Marshall and I had the opportunity to see how each of these many churches operated. The more Marshall saw and heard, the more convinced he was that too many conservative Christians have a destructive wait-and-see attitude. Not just in Texas, but in every state we heard the same theme: "We're in the last days. Jesus will rapture us at any time and take us away from all of this."

Marshall liked to challenge this. "What about living right now and gathering together as one body and doing something about the air and water pollution? How about taking time to pick up some of the litter along the streets? What about the teenagers who are our future doctors, lawyers, politicians, farmers? Have you noticed that the U.S. has the highest rate of teenage suicide in the world?"

No, generally people admitted that they didn't know anything about teen suicide. And they didn't seem to want to know, either. "It's too bad, but what can we do about it?" was the prevailing attitude.

Marshall kept talking. "Have you heard the statement President Kennedy made: 'Ask not what your country can do for you, but what you can do for your country.'?" And in case they needed to hear it from the Bible, Marshall added, "From what I understand, Jesus said, 'Occupy until I come.'" (see Luke 19:13).

This conversation occurred repeatedly. There was an overall lackadaisical, careless spirit that Marshall and I noticed as we walked.

In our early morning prayers, we asked God to obliterate division and carelessness that Satan had placed on the body of Christ; we prayed that the peace, love, and harmony of Jesus Christ would manifest itself in the church. As we traveled, we thanked God whenever we noticed evidence that walls were coming down.

For most of the rest of the trip across Texas, we were able to stay overnight in homes. In Wheeler, our hosts were a young couple whose teenage daughter had just died from an overdose of drugs.

The father and mother, who had married as teenagers, were overcome with grief and shared their story with us. Their red-haired, freckle-faced only child had been happy and carefree. But in junior-high, she had started to withdraw. Both parents had worked long hours and their latch-key daughter had watched whatever she wanted on television when she got home. Popping aspirin had graduated to popping her mothers' Valium. Then she began to drink small amounts of her dad's vodka, mixed with orange juice. "She was such a sweet, innocent child, and I was so busy," said her mother, Gayle, "I just didn't notice how quiet she had become. I thought she was going through a stage. On her thirteenth birthday she seemed to have grown up overnight.

"She still looked like a child; we didn't realize she was having older boys over and having pot parties after school. A neighbor spotted an older boy leaving the house in a hurry. When I got home from work, she was lying on the couch curled up in a fetal position. I went over to wake her up. She wasn't asleep; she was dead. Our only child," she cried, rocking back and forth. Her husband tried to comfort her, but she was crying so hard no one could reach her.

Marshall and I silently prayed and wept in our hearts. It was all we could do. We tried to plant some seeds, to tell this couple that Jesus wants to carry our griefs and sorrows. But this couple wasn't ready. We left their home quietly, still praying for them in silence.

Generally, our hosts were Christians. Our Sunday morning and evening ministry in churches was a link, a grapevine, that had spread from one stop to the next. Pastor and parishioners in one town would refer us to someone in the next. They would give us a name to call or they would make the contact themselves and say, "You've heard about Bob Wieland walking on his hands? Bob and Marshall are coming this way. Do you know any home that would be open to them?" Someone would say, "Sure." We considered this a miracle that we never took for granted.

Sometimes Marshall would go ahead and check out the logistics. If someone said we were welcome, he'd go check the place out. Some homes were out-of-the-way—and some were simply inadequate. Marshall had a graceful way of declining invitations. If a situation looked fine, we often stayed several weeks, commuting to our locations on the highway. The homes usually were about sixty miles apart. When we'd get thirty miles out of town, we'd move on to the next, thirty miles ahead of us.

I put everything I had into the walk. And I settled into a routine with Marshall. In the morning, we ate cereal, either All-Bran or old fashioned oatmeal with raisins and skim milk. I would start walking somewhere between 8:30 and 9:00 A.M. I would walk until about one, when we would stop for lunch. If there was a restaurant close by, we might go in, but usually Marshall brought out whole-wheat bread and a slice of cheese. We would drink apple or orange juice, and then, after a little rest, I'd walk again until seven, sometimes even a little later if the sun was still up. By that time I felt totally spent.

So many gracious hosts wanted to invite us out to eat here or there. We simply had to let them know that we found it difficult to run around to different homes. Most evenings we ate in the home where we were staying. I normally ate what they set before me, but my favorite food was and is spaghetti. I love spaghetti—and vegetables, fruit, and lots of water. I tried to go to bed early. Most of the time I didn't feel I could sit up and visit, as I had to keep up my strength. So Marshall and I didn't do any entertaining; sometimes we didn't even have time to be entertained.

All across Texas, the hospitality was outstanding. Once we attended a good ol' family reunion; it was an old-fashioned, Fourth-of-July barbecue with some of the best steak I've ever eaten. Five generations gathered together from all corners of the United States to break bread, show off their children, and get to know one another better.

There was plenty of good talk—and food: corn on the cob, potato salads, macaroni salads, fragrant homemade bread. There were so many American flags flying in the breeze to celebrate the Fourth that the patriotic feeling nearly overwhelmed me. The flag reminded me of everything America stands for—freedom, the right to worship where I choose, the right to speak my mind. America—sweet land of liberty—my home!

After the barbecue a band played "God Bless America" and "The Battle Hymn of the Republic while red, white, and blue fireworks—more spectacular than Disneyland—exploded overhead. It was a Fourth of July I would remember for a long, long time.

One summer day, Marshall had a surprise visitor: his attractive twenty-nine-year-old daughter, "Jay Nine," as he called her, appeared with a girlfriend who called Marshall "Sing-Along," for obvious reasons. I'd never seen Marshall so happy. He had admitted that he missed his kids, and Jay Nine and her friend accompanied us for several days before they headed north.

On the weekends, we ministered in churches. Normally we ate the Sunday noon meal with the pastor and then spoke again at a Sunday evening service.

Marshall always found the best places to visit, including the white-domed McDonald Observatory at Fort Davis and the

Shafter ghost town, a silver-mining town that had been mined out in 1942.

"Hey, Bob," he said, "what do you say, shall we go back and mine the tunnels? An old miner I met there said there's still some silver back in there."

I looked at Marshall. His eyes were smiling, as usual. "Sure, why not?" I agreed, kidding him back. "We can donate the proceeds to World Vision and the Red Cross!"

Before leaving Texas, Marshall decided to visit the Monahans Sandhills State Park, known for its golden dunes, which rise up over seventy feet above the flat landscape. Unfortunately, Marshall arrived during a sand storm and nearly got blown away.

And I nearly got blown away about that same time, although by a different kind of storm. One day I stepped off to the side of the road to avoid some construction. It was just starting to rain heavily. The ground beside the road looked stable, but it was as oozy as quicksand.

Thank God that Marshall was nearby. I yelled and he rushed over to me. But he slipped and soon we were both scrambling around like muddy snowmen. It took some doing even with Marshall's expert help to get me out. For a moment I just sat on the side of the road and contemplated the mud. We were safe, but what a clean-up job that was!

What a way to remember Texas!

12

OKLAHOMA: YOU CAN WIN!

Late in August 1984 we entered Oklahoma, where the wind rushes down the plain and churns up dust and some of the most awesome tumbleweeds I've ever seen. We quickly discovered that Oklahomans have their own special brand of hospitality. Home after home opened to us, and speaking engagements opened doors for Christ.

For part of our time in Oklahoma, we stayed with a silver-haired woman, Emily Tyler, who loved to rock in her cane-backed chair on the front porch. She would read her Bible for a while, then stop to knit or crochet.

I felt peaceful around her. Emily loved to bake bread, cookies, and muffins for the nearby nursing home. Every Sunday and Wednesday night, she would gather up her Bible and baked goods and head for the nursing home. One Sunday evening Marshall and I went with her to give our testimonies. Marshall was asked to lead a sing-along.

"Go ahead, Marshall," I teased, "hymns are your middle name." Marshall good-naturedly introduced himself as Sing-Along Cardiff. We had a great time. After we read the Word, gave our testimonies, and sang along with Sing-Along, we bobbed for apples and enjoyed Emily's cookies.

"You know, Emily is almost ninety years old," said one of the residents, confidently.

"Really?" I said.

"You know why she stays so young?" asked the old, bent man.

"No, why?"

"Because she doesn't eat too much of her own cooking!"

"No, that's not why," said the woman next to him. "It's because she helps other folks, that's why." Emily was a giver.

During our time at her house, Marshall took off to visit the Alabaster Caverns State Park in Freedom. *Oh, no,* I thought to myself, *he must be in geological heaven. I bet he'll hit me with some more geology lessons when he comes back.*

Sure enough, bright and early the next morning he asked me, "Hey, Bob, do you know what alabaster's made of?"

"No, Marshall, what's alabaster made of?"

"It's a fine translucent gypsum."

He went on to describe the two-thousand-foot-long cavern formation containing huge deposits of gypsum.

"You should see the crystal formations, Bob! They're fantastic!"

"That's why I have you, Marshall, so I can walk and see at the same time."

I really did wonder what I would do without him.

Marshall and I spoke at a prison outside of Oklahoma City. I will always remember the prisoners' reactions when I opened my talk by standing on my stumps in my wheelchair and saying, "I'd like to ask you a question. Has anybody been going through a hard time lately? I hear some of you think you have problems." Some of them actually looked down at their legs, maybe checking to make sure they were still there.

I knew that some of them would be released on probation soon. They'd have a chance to start a new life, walk out as free men. I knew that prisoners who received Jesus were more likely to stay out of prison when they got out. My prayer for them was that they would walk out as free men in Jesus Christ, the One who sets people free indeed.

Marshall and I thanked God that we had been used as

channels to bring scores of inmates to the Lord. I hoped that
there would be further studies of the Word in the prison, as
ignorance of the Bible is one reason so many people fall away.

Later, as we walked by the prison, many of the prisoners
watched us from the yard. Since they weren't supposed to talk
to anybody outside the fence, they gave me hand signals that
said, "Right on, brother."

I felt as if they were giving me a gift. I had given them a shot
of positive energy, and they were returning it back to me,
sending me on my way east with a boost of power.

About that time Marshall began the second phase of my
education: horticulture. As we traveled past farms he'd say,
"Hey, Bob, what kind of crop is that?"

I'd fall for his line like a fish for bait. "Soy?"

"No, it's a golden maize crop."

"What's a golden maize crop?" I'd ask.

He'd leave me hanging for a few steps, then reply, "It's a
cornfield, Bob. Surprised you didn't know that one."

Weeks later, by the time we neared Tulsa, summer had
turned to winter, and we found out that it snows in Oklahoma.
One morning after a stormy night, our hosts Senator and Mrs.
John Young, graciously made arrangements for a snowplow to
clear a path for Marshall and me to walk on. The snow path
was cleared for three or four miles, the distance I anticipated I
would walk that day. It was smooth sailing!

During our morning prayer sessions, Marshall and I prayed
from John 16:24, "Ask and you will receive, and your joy will be
complete." One of the things we asked for was excellent
weather conditions, and our prayers were answered. We were
able to avoid most of the severe storms that came through.

The coldest weather, however, was at Vinita, Oklahoma.
With a wind-chill factor of twenty-six degrees below zero, the
schools were closed, and I never realized how cold winter
could be. It seemed as if my breath formed icicles as I spoke to
Marshall. The chill went all the way into my bones.

Sometimes people would comment that it was God's will for
there to be violent, destructive weather, like a tornado that kills
scores of people. "Not true!" I said. "Satan has come to kill and

destroy using any means, just as he tried to kill me in
Vietnam." God promises seventy healthy years, not that our
lives would be snuffed out in a hurricane or tornado or fire
(Psalm 90:10).

One of those severe storms I missed was as I was driving
home to California from Tulsa. This was the last time I drove
back to see Jackey, and I was so eager to get there, I drove
twenty-nine hours—straight through. I knew that from then
on I'd have to fly home. This was ridiculous. When I returned
to Oklahoma, I found out that I'd just missed a blinding storm
that had wreaked havoc on the roads.

In Tulsa I was delighted to be reunited with Larry Cochell,
one of my fellow faculty members at Cal State, L.A. He was
now head baseball coach and athletic director at Oral Roberts
University. I had worked out with his baseball team at Cal
State. Larry and I talked "old times" and reconstructed some of
the great major league baseball plays of previous years. As
often as I could, I caught the big games on television. I was
always willing to talk through a game with an interested party.

Larry had arranged for me to talk to the students of O.R.U.
Speaking to college and high school students has been one of
my most fulfilling experiences. Almost every student in every
part of America and Canada has made me feel more than
welcome. They've let me know that my message contributed to
their lives, that they appreciated the time I spent with them.

I shared my testimony and how my faith in the Lord Jesus
Christ had enabled me to do all that God had called me to do.

After my talk, I had the chance to talk personally with some
of the students. They were typical of kids all across America.
So many high school and college students expressed concern
about the future. What would things be like when they were
out of school? Some O.R.U. students said how grateful they
were that, knowing Jesus as their personal Lord and Savior,
they knew they had a Protector and a Covering no matter what
the future held.

Richard Roberts, Oral's son, also invited me to be a guest on
his show, "Richard Roberts Live," to share my testimony and
the reason why I was walking across America.

I think Marshall sometimes wondered why we were doing
this, especially when sponsors we thought we'd lined up to
support the walk didn't follow through. Fortunately, when one
door closed, another always opened up. Whenever we were
low on funds, we, like the lilies of the field, were fed and
clothed. We never missed a meal and were even able to
accumulate love offerings that we later sent to organizations
such as the American Red Cross and World Vision to help feed
the hungry.

During my walk, the "We are the World" event and song
caught the attention of the media and the public. Millions of
dollars were raised to help feed the hungry. "We Are the
World" was followed by Band Aid, Live Aid, Farm Aid, and
Hands Across America. All of these media events raised large
amounts of money.

I like to think that perhaps the Spirit of America publicity
had helped to inspire the first record and video, "We Are the
World." A number of people we met along the way also felt
that our walk was like the first domino in a chain reaction. I
hoped so.

Before we left Oklahoma we were invited to speak at a high
school assembly in a small town that hadn't won a football
game in years. Marshall encouraged me, "Come on Bob, you
can do it. You know you're good for at least two touchdowns.
Give it to them!"

At first the students didn't seem as receptive to the Strive for
Success assembly as had kids in most of the schools we'd
previously visited.

As I shared my testimony and did my weight-lifting demon-
strations, I had to work extra hard to generate enthusiasm.
Half-way into my talk, showing the students a dummy eighty-
two-millimeter mortar round, of the kind that blew off my legs
in Vietnam, I dropped it on the floor—just to see if I could get
a reaction out of them. I often use this trick to get a rise out of
kids. Normally they jump or show some reaction. Not this
group; no one moved a muscle. "Hey, anyone alive out there?"
I asked. No response!

"You see, when you get hit with one of these babies, it can

ruin your whole day!" Again I looked for a sign of life. "How many of you enjoy breathing?" I asked. Maybe 5 percent raised their hands. "Say, I have a thought. Maybe you're not getting enough oxygen out there?" A few of the girls giggled.

I did my hand stand on the trampoline. Dead silence. No wonder this football team always lost. They needed help!

When I told them about winning the United States Power-lifting Championships bantam-weight title and having it snatched away, the group began to sit up straight. "You know," I said, "my dad and my grandfather taught me it's better to try and try again and keep failing than not to try at all."

Right then the students woke up, at least their eyes were open. "Yeh, it's a fact. The most successful people have failed more often than the average person. There really are no successes or failures in life, just experience! How many believe you can win the game tonight? Raise your hand if you believe you can win."

A few of the football players and the coaches half-heartedly raised their hands. "Hey, I'm not talking to just the players and the coaches. I'm talking to the team. You all are the team!" All of a sudden that spirit, the Spirit of America, whooshed into the room. "Do you believe we can win?" A loud roar filled the auditorium.

One of the cheerleaders yelled, "Go, team, go!" Soon every kid in the room was shouting, "We're going to win. We're going to win!"

I finished with, "Go out and win one. You can do it!"

And they did. For the first time in its history, the team won by two touchdowns.

"Bob, I told you, you could do it!" Marshall said.

"Hey, you know it was team effort," I responded. Just like my walk.

13

MISSOURI: SHOW ME, SO GOD DID!

Walking across the state line between Oklahoma and Missouri seemed like climbing a wall between two countries. Oklahoma had been so hospitable. At first some of the Missourians seemed to be living in a world of their own. Marshall and I had more problems finding homes open to us there than in any other place. When we first walked into Missouri, we didn't know where we'd stay, until Marshall visited First Assembly of God in Joplin. Petite, gray-haired Lola Diggs was a secretary there. She listened to Marshall tell our story. As Marshall was ready to leave, she called him back and said, "Would you like to stay in our home?" Yes, we would, thank you!

Lola's husband, Richard, was in the same line of work as Marshall—irrigation and water use. He was one of the most prolific inventors in the country, with more than one hundred inventions patented in one year. His mind was always going a mile a minute.

Both Richard and Lola were great encouragers. Lola came out and walked with us for several days. While we were staying with the Diggses, a middle-aged, fair-haired, slender man named Bob Philips and his honey-haired young daughter, Kelly, stopped on the highway to ask if there was anything they could do to help. Bob was a control engineer who ministered in nursing homes on weekends and acted in a local theater company. A dedicated family man, he and his wife, Paula, had four children who really loved the Lord. Kelly had heard me speak at her school and had suggested that her dad bring her out to meet me. The Philipses contributed to the Spirit of America and said they would see us again.

Outside of Joplin I felt a definite tug from the Holy Spirit to change my planned route. We were walking Interstate 44, and I said to Marshall, "I just feel led to get off this highway and go on the parallel state road about seven miles over to the north."

Marshall had his own opinion. "Bob, that's a two-day journey out of your way. We'll never get to Washington if we start getting off course like this." He seemed a little bit perturbed, but I felt strongly.

"I just feel the Lord would have me go that way, and I want to be obedient."

Marshall understood. "Well, if the Lord told you to do it, let's do it."

So we walked up the parallel road. About three days later, a large, powerfully built man drove by in his car, stopped, and walked back to encourage me. He was a Vietnam vet, he said, from my division, the Twenty-fifth Infantry. We reminisced a few moments about Vietnam. Eager to keep going, I didn't want to talk very long. "Well, I got to go," I said. I thanked him for stopping, said good-bye, and started walking again.

A little while later this same guy ran toward me, waving a scrapbook he'd gone back home to find. "Bob," he said, "look at these pictures I took in Nam and see if you recognize anyone?" Though I still wanted to be on my way, I looked at the first page—and recognized one of the Viet Cong we'd captured. Then I said, "Well, what do you know? There's Ralph."

The man stared right at me for a few moments and then said, "Doc?"

From somewhere in the back of my mind I recognized his voice: "Dennis!"

Talk about divine appointment, being sent to the right place at the right time! I could hardly believe it! I was standing on the street talking to Dennis Cooper, my Vietnam buddy. I probably hadn't recognized him because he'd gained about eighty pounds. We laughed and cried and hugged. We talked about the day of my accident, and as he spoke, I made an incredible discovery. The unknown soldier whose quick thinking and actions had saved my life was Dennis. The overwhelming joy I felt was beyond words.

Dennis was still married. His son, born while Dennis was in Vietnam, was now a teenager. Dennis also had two daughters, and he worked with school kids. His big size seemed to match his big heart. I also learned that David Denier, our point man, lived near Dennis. Later that day we had a regular reunion.

Dennis and I spent long hours getting caught up, and Marshall and I talked again and again about the lesson we'd learned about obeying God's voice. "Just think, if I had had my way, you would have missed Dennis," Marshall said solemnly.

When we walked far enough out of Joplin that it wasn't practical to return to the Diggs's home at night, we said our farewells to Lola and Richard. They'd been good to us, even packing us a lunch the day we left. Not long after we left, Marshall and I learned that the Diggs's factory had burned down. It seemed that Satan had used one of Richard and Lola's trusted acquaintances to set the blaze. And yet the Lord opened the door for them to get another factory operating quickly. In human terms, the Diggses lost a lot. But time and time again I've seen that God, according to Scripture, will return that which has been stolen. He is the Great Restorer.

On one bright spring day in the Ozarks, Marshall and I enjoyed a picnic of whole wheat bread, white cheese, and apples. Marshall pointed to a tree and started to play his game. "Bob, what kind of tree do you think that is?"

I checked it out and saw that a pail dangled from one side of it. I was quite sure I knew what that meant.

"It's a maple."

"No, not a maple. It's a Rubrum tree."

Just as we were picking up our picnic and leaving, a farmer came by and checked out the tree. "Pardon me sir, but what kind of a tree is that?" I asked.

"Why it's a maple, and I'm collecting sap to make syrup," he replied.

I turned to Marshall who was smiling. "Ah-ha," I said, "it *is* a maple tree."

"Trick question," he said.

I could never win.

At least Marshall's questions and lessons kept his mind off some of the everyday mechanics and made the trip more exciting.

The homes we stayed in were from sixty to seventy miles apart. Our next stop was in Springfield, where we stayed with Bill and Nadine Britan, long-time residents of Springfield and friends of my secretary, Margaret Harvey. We stayed in the third story of their home, and I climbed the steps on my hands. When you walk several miles a day on your hands, what are a few stairs?

In downtown Springfield, a prosperous looking man stepped out of a big, beautiful automobile and introduced himself as Frank Douglas, owner of the local Howard Johnson Motel. He held out keys and said, "Here are your room numbers. We've already got two rooms reserved for you. We also want you to have your meals with us."

We discovered that we had a choice of seven restaurants! "Just give the room clerk your room number and charge your meal to your room," the manager said. When we completed our stay at the Britans, we did stay at Howard Johnson's, where the manager got the whole staff of one hundred together so we could speak to them.

Across the state, Chaplain Lewis made arrangements for us to spend a "homecoming week" at Fort Leonard Wood, where I had trained for Vietnam combat.

The chaplain arranged for me to speak to the troops in the big field house. I felt such a bond of friendship with the men. To introduce my testimony, I shared some of my experiences in boot camp: I'd come so close to being a cook instead of a medic. I said, "When I came home minus my legs, some of my friends suggested that I should have learned to cook.

"I always said, 'No, if I had to do it over again, I'd go, and willingly. It's a great honor to serve your country, and I was proud to go. What's more, I was overjoyed to come home A.O.A.—alive on arrival, not D.O.A.'"

There was a respectful silence and then applause. The men could identify with that. I continued my testimony, which was interspersed with a lot of laughter, applause, yelling, and cheering.

In 1969 I had left the base, heading straight for combat. Now, fifteen years later, I was hopeful that these soldiers would not see the horrors of real war. I prayed that God would spare them.

When we'd "outwalked" our base at Fort Leonard Wood, we moved our baggage to Eureka, outside of St. Louis. There we stayed with Rich Richl and his wife, Carla, a Christian gospel singer. Rich recorded Carla's music, which she used to minister to others. Tall, statuesque Carla walked with me several days, serenading me with her unique voice and original songs. She sang at several of my speaking engagements, including a women's prison.

Rich, Carla, Marshall, and I enjoyed some deep spiritual discussions and great fellowship. I felt a special kinship with this couple and suspected that we'd see more of each other when the walk was over. Was there some way their ministry would mesh with mine? I was sad to say good-bye to them but delighted that we were at last approaching the Mississippi. When we crossed it, we would be on a last leg of the journey.

Was I excited to see the arch that rises up over the St. Louis skyline, the Gateway to the West—or to the East if you're coming from the West! The arch seemed like a sunrise to me, a promise of new ventures. Maybe it was the reminder of the pioneers crossing over that old man river into the unknown wilds that spurred me on, made me eager to "go east, young man, go east."

In St. Louis, we stayed with the Renolettes, who lived near the Arch. We relaxed in their spacious living room, high up, surrounded by glass windows. Looking out one of the glass-walled windows, we could see the St. Louis Arch, the ships on the Mississippi, and the magical lights of the city. As we sat there, Marshall casually remarked that things were pretty calm, not much excitement recently. At those words, Teddy Renolette and his wife, Charlene, looked at each other and said that things hadn't always been as placid as they seemed now. Recently, they had nearly lost their lives.

Teddy said, "Charlene and I and our daughter were enjoying a quiet evening at home, when three masked men broke into the living room. It was like a scene from a cops-and-robbers TV program, except where were the cops?

"'Hands up,' one said, as my chihuahua shivered in fright at my feet.

"The thought crossed my mind that he was going to kill me. *Oh, my God, I'm going to die! What about my wife and daughter? I can't die; I have to protect them.*

"'Hands up,' one man screamed. 'I mean it; I'll kill you!'

"The robber threatened me as he began to shoot in the floor." Teddy pointed to the floor. "That's where the first bullet hit." I looked at Marshall. He had the most incredulous look on his face, as Teddy continued. "The guy aimed straight at my heart. I tried to protect my face and my heart. As I put my arms up, I heard a gun go off. I was hit in the temple. As I fell to the floor, I pulled at his mask and was shocked to discover that robber number one was a vagrant I had hired to work in one of my eight gas stations.

"Next, he hit me with a pipe wrench. One of the robbers went directly to the office where we counted our proceeds from our business. Charlene managed to escape and hide behind a rocking chair.

"My son-in-law, who lived in the apartment adjoining our house, heard the commotion and came running in, holding his gun. But when the robbers saw my son-in-law, they decided to leave in a hurry. I know that angels were present as we were really in darkness. The room lit up like sunshine.

"The robbers tried to take our daughter as a hostage on the way out. She grabbed a door knob and was given supernatural strength to hold on. Eleven shots were fired before they escaped. It's a miracle any of us are still alive.

"The man we identified was arrested on several counts: aggravated battery, attempted murder, robbery, and so on.

"After they left, my family and I thanked the Lord, and my wife read Psalm 27:

> "The Lord is my light and my salvation—
> whom shall I fear?
> The Lord is the stronghold of my life—
> of whom shall I be afraid?
> When evil men advance against me
> to devour my flesh,
> when my enemies and my foes attack me,
> they will stumble and fall.
> Though an army besiege me,
> my heart will not fear;
> though war break out against me,
> even then will I be confident."

Marshall and I were very quiet; we were stunned. As we got ready for bed, I said, trying to cheer Marshall up, "Not enough excitement, huh, Marshall? I think I like things just the way they are."

The next day Teddy explained that the robbery in many ways was a blessing in disguise. "I had become proud; my business was doing well. It took this kind of shock to wake me up and take stock of my life. Right after the robbery I felt I should retire and go into the ministry full time."

Marshall and I knew that once God calls you into His service, you need to obey immediately.

14

ILLINOIS: LOST AND FOUND

Maybe Marshall too had been influenced by the sight of the great arch and the Mississippi River. Right after we'd crossed the divide, as we were walking through East St. Louis, he became quiet. His usual peace was gone, replaced by a churning undercurrent of discontent. For a day or so I let it pass, then I felt I should speak up.

"Marshall, what's wrong?" I asked. "Is something bothering you?"

"Yes, there is, but I prefer not to talk about it," Marshall replied.

"C'mon, Marshall, we're buddies, you can tell me."

It took some coaxing before he finally spoke his mind. "Well, it's like this, Bob. This trip is taking longer than I expected. We're nowhere near Washington."

Here I was so delighted that we were in the east, and Marshall was thinking about how far we had to go before we got to our goal! He was right, of course. I remembered telling Jackey that this trip would take a year, maybe two. I'd been out now for two-and-a-half years, and we were just two-thirds of the way across the continent.

"Marshall, are you trying to tell me you want to quit?"

"No, I'm not a quitter," he said; then he walked for a mile in silence.

In my spirit I knew that Marshall was my man—the one God wanted to stay with me all the way to our last goal. I prayed hard during that mile, asking God to give His peace to Marshall. I knew he'd be miserable if he didn't believe in his heart that he was doing the right thing. Finally I said, "Marshall, it's okay if you want to turn back."

"No, I don't want to turn back," he said.

"Let's just drop it."

I didn't pursue the issue anymore. But I was confident that Marshall would stay to the end. He was a man of his word.

We had been warned to be careful in East St. Louis, since parts of the town were dangerous, like parts of almost every large town we passed through. We prayed for God's protection, of course, but we were also careful to take precautionary measures. As we walked from the city out into the suburbs and then the countryside, we thanked God that we'd received nothing but respect from the people of East St. Louis. Even some bikers, dressed in black leather and sporting beards, stopped to contribute to the "Walk" and see what else they could do to help. I learned a long time ago not to judge appearances.

Actually, even the canine population east of St. Louis was kinder than I had expected. One evening, near dark, I walked toward a house with a Doberman pinscher sitting on the front porch. He looked like the kind that would attack any passerby and let his owner ask questions later. I prayed to get past this serious black dog in one piece. But just as I walked directly in front of the house, I—and the dog—heard barking in the backyard. In a flash he was up and gone to investigate something more interesting than I. Phew, I could breathe freely again, until the next threat—which came from a quieter, slower source.

When Marshall and I had traveled Interstate 70 for quite a distance we noticed a number of turtles of different sizes splattered on the highway. There were many lakes nearby, and it looked as if the turtles had decided to take a stroll. They would have been of only passing interest if I hadn't suddenly come eyeball to eyeball with the largest snapping turtle I had ever seen. He must have weighed fifty pounds!

Ironically, I'd often thought of myself as a tortoise who plodded along, winning the race by perseverance. Now I was faced with the real thing—a General Patton of a turtle, bulldozing his way toward me. I felt as if I were no match for him; he looked as if he meant business. I did not know at the time that these guys could bite off fingers or even a hand—but he had a dangerous look in his eye.

The highway's shoulder was quite narrow at that point, obviously not big enough for both of us. It would be dangerous for either the turtle or me to step into the traffic, though the turtle had no intention of going anywhere other than straight ahead. He kept moving toward me like a tank. A showdown was imminent. When I lifted my size-one running shoes and tried to move him off the road, he snapped. I got out of his way, but tried again. Pretty soon we were dueling it out on the highway. Here was an irresistible force meeting an immovable object (though I don't know which was which). This turtle just kept on moving ahead, all systems go.

Finally, Marshall, who had been walking far behind me, caught up and got in on the fray. He somehow managed to move the turtle down an embankment, away from the traffic—and away from me.

Soon after our encounter with the turtle, an Illinois highway patrolman stopped to ask if there was anything he could do to assist us. We introduced ourselves, explained our goal, and said we were doing just fine—as long as we didn't run into any more Illinois turtles. The police were exceptionally kind and supportive. Two officers even invited us home for dinner.

The farther we traveled across the heart of America, the more we realized how necessary the police and highway patrol are to the safety of travelers.

One day after another highway patrolman had stopped to see if we needed assistance, we noticed an abandoned, six-month-old German shepherd lying in a ditch. At first I thought he was dead, maybe hit by a car. Marshall went to check him out and the pup rolled over and opened an eye—very much alive, though hungry and dehydrated. "He was playing dead, Marshall, just to check us out."

Bolstered up by some water and food, he was soon walking with us, like a Spirit of America mascot. One more dog had "fallen in my lap," claimed me as its own. Jackey would get a laugh out of this, because on one of my trips home, while I waited in the car with the window open as she shopped, from out of nowhere a beige French poodle had jumped in the window. She landed, plop, in my lap, almost taking my breath away, and she had wiggled around, just asking for love and affection.

When Jackey returned, she fell in love with her, so we'd kept her and named her Sugar. And now another one, a German shepherd, had taken a liking to me. Well, one more dog mouth to feed wouldn't make much difference. . . .

But Marshall and I agreed that Interstate 70 wasn't any place to raise a black-and-tan shepherd pup. There were hazards worse than snapping turtles. Marshall recalled the two semis that had recently raced past as if they were drag cars. The one closest to the shoulder—and us—must have been going ninety miles an hour—and did we scramble fast!

The nameless pup stayed for several days. "Marshall," I said, "do you think he jumped out of a car window? He's obviously lost, and he's out here in the middle of nowhere."

"We'll probably never know, but we'd better find him a home pretty quick. We can't keep him."

Soon we found a family with a small boy to adopt the puppy. I know he got a good home—as good a home as Jackey would have made for him if she'd laid eyes on him.

That pup wasn't the only "lost" one Marshall and I found on the Illinois highways. One day when we were driving the motorcycle toward a high school rally, we noticed two fourteen- or fifteen-year-old girls up ahead, hitchhiking. Dressed in punker style, they carried a portable radio, which blared heavy-metal rock loud enough to be heard in Indiana.

Marshall leaned over and whispered in my ear. The dark-haired girl looked like a picture on a missing-person poster he'd just seen. As we got closer, he grew more convinced. "Bob, I'm sure about the one on the left," he said. So we stopped.

As we approached, they started walking away, as if they had something to hide. "Slow down," I said, "we just want to see if we can help you." The red-haired, freckle-faced teenager whispered to her brunette friend.

"Okay, but how come you stopped?" said the dark-haired girl whose voice seemed very deep for a teenager.

"Yeah," said the petite red-head, "you don't have no room on your cycle for us. You can't give us a ride—so what do you want?"

"We want to help you if we can," said Marshall.

"You look lost. Are you?" I asked.

"None of your business," said Red.

The brunette got right to the point: "You said you wanted to help. We need money. You have any? We'll pay you back, we promise."

"How?" Marshall asked in a most fatherly voice.

The girls explained that they were actresses in Chicago, starring in x-rated films. With some coaxing, they told us more of their story. The red-haired girl was twelve and the brunette, eleven. The brunette, who did most of the talking, said that when her divorced mother had found out what her daughter had been doing, she'd kicked her out of the house. Then when she'd had second thoughts, she'd called the police. Both girls had just been put on the missing-persons list. Being wanted by both the police and the Chicago producers they worked for, they had decided to run away to Los Angeles and break into the movies, big time.

We tried to reason with them. They simply weren't safe. We explained their options. They could give us a parent's name and number, or since they were minors, we would call the police.

Red, who said her name was Penny, began to cry like the child she was. She willingly gave us her dad's phone number. Together, we all made our way to the nearest pay phone. I called her father and he promised to come right away and to call the other girl's mother. We agreed to meet them later at the high school where I was to speak that afternoon.

Just at that moment, one of the teachers we knew at that school happened to drive by, noticed us, and stopped. She gave the girls and me a lift to the school, and Marshall followed on his motorcycle. At the end of my talk, they both received the Lord—two prodigal daughters come home. We said good-bye to them and their parents, praying that God would nourish them with the milk and bread of His Word.

Not far from the Indiana border we suddenly found ourselves in the midst of family problems of a different kind. We were staying with a family who had kindly invited us to their home while we were passing through the area. They were kind and generous to us. But while washing up for dinner one evening, Marshall and I overheard the wife loudly accusing her husband of having an affair with the woman next door.

"That's a lie," he replied. "Who's been saying these things?"

"The woman across the street said she saw you."

"Well, she's lying," said the husband.

At dinner, the wife asked us to pray for their marriage. Her husband then began to complain that she was trying to wear the pants in the family, that she was making all the decisions and spending the money, to which she replied, "As long as I make most of the money, I'll help decide how we spend it!"

Marshall and I knew that only spiritual intervention could save this marriage. We talked to them about God's view of divorce and how important forgiveness is in any relationship. Skeptical, the wife asked Marshall how he knew: "Are you married?"

"Yes," he admitted. "I was married for many years. I have two beautiful daughters and a son. I'm a grandfather three times over."

"Well, where's your wife?" the woman asked.

He paused a moment and said, "She's . . . gone."

The woman said, "Oh, I'm so sorry."

After that we enjoyed a great spaghetti dinner and some wonderfully light-hearted conversation. Everything seemed to be going well; the family was laughing together and enjoying our company. *Just maybe*, I thought, *in some small way, we have helped this couple avoid a divorce.*

The next day, however, when we returned from walking, we found the wife in the kitchen, crying. She handed us a note. Her husband had left her—for the woman next door.

We felt so helpless. We had witnessed much joy and harmony in the Christian homes we had stayed in, but we also saw the strife and pain that exist in many families all across the country. Parents were fighting with children; husbands and wives were giving up on their marriages. It was a sobering reminder of every family's need for Jesus Christ.

15

INDIANA: REACHING AMERICA'S KIDS

In August 1985 we left Illinois. As we entered Terre Haute, Indiana, we quickly discovered why Indiana is known for "Hoosier Hospitality." Most of the Hoosiers we met were warm and friendly.

A few kids, however, gave us a cool welcome. As we traveled on Route 40 past Terre Haute, an interesting scenic route, we were staying with the Jacksons. One weekend we went back to St. Louis for a speaking engagement. While we were gone, some kids broke into the Jacksons' garage and took Marshall's bicycle. Actually, our hosts were more upset about the loss than either Marshall or I. What concerned us more was the great need of these teenagers who seemed more destructive than in my generation. Something had to shake these teen-agers up before their evil-doings reached more epidemic proportions.

I was doing what I could to feed God's Word to as many teenagers as possible. I remember one particular assembly at a high school in Indianapolis, where I related my experience in Vietnam, my adjustments to losing my legs, and my weight-lifting career. I explained how, with God's help, I overcame the challenges; we are more than conquerors, through the overwhelming love of Jesus Christ. "God has proven to me that

His promises are true," I said as I did my weight-lifting demonstration. "I also learned that life is precious. Each breath I breathe—or you breathe—is more precious than rubies, diamonds, silver, or gold. Physical life is temporary. That's why it's important to do the best we can and to appreciate *every* moment."

I couldn't tell if I was getting my message across—that life is beautiful, no matter what the circumstances. But after I completed my talk, a shy-looking student came up to me. I shook his hand and asked his name. "Robert Larson," he answered, "a sophomore." He thanked me for the talk. Then he pulled a shiny medal out of his pocket. "Here," he said, "I want you to have this."

It was a souvenir medal from the 1984 Olympics. When one of his classmates saw what Robert had given me, the boy privately told me, "That medal's his most prized possession. He carries it with him everywhere, you know. Not long ago he tried to commit suicide. You must have really reached him."

I held the medal in my hand and thought about the teenager and his "most prized" possession. I prayed for Robert and all of the other students, hoping they understood what I had learned in Vietnam: Life is our most prized possession and we should never waste a moment of it or take it for granted.

Most of the time we were well received when we spoke. One late afternoon, right before Halloween, a reporter got out of her car, walked over to us, and enthusiastically said, "I've been keeping up with your walk, and I'd like to do an article, front page, about your journey."

Marshall acted as my P.R. person, acting on my behalf, and said, "That'll be great. You can call us. We're staying at Mr. Ryan's house. The number is in the book."

The reporter, Annie Heyman, and I got together, and she did an interview focusing on our walk through Indiana.

The night after the interview she called. "Bob, I'm going to have to shorten your article to get it and your picture on the front page."

"Fine," I said. "Sounds great."

The next night she called again. "Bob, I'm sorry to tell you, but I not only had to shorten your article, I had to move it to the second page and eliminate your picture."

"Oh?" I said.

"Yes," she replied. "We had to replace your story with a news break."

I knew that second page wasn't half bad. "That's okay," I assured her. "Thanks for your interest."

The next day I read the paper, which gave me a good laugh, because there on the front page was a picture of a giant pumpkin and a story about the local Halloween festivities. Imagine, the walk had been upstaged by a pumpkin!

On our way toward Indianapolis, a man parked his car and approached us. Because he wore a VFW hat, I thought it likely that he was a World War II veteran.

"Hi, I'm Paul Beutell," he said. "I've been looking all over for you, and finally, I found a highway patrolman who led me to you."

"Well, what can we do for you?" Marshall asked.

What a welcome response: "I just felt I should come and encourage you and see what I can do to help you."

And indeed, Paul and his wife, Catherine, turned out to be very helpful. I was right. Paul was a vet, having served with the Army's One-hundredth Infantry Division in France and Germany. Radio and television had been his field, and he now owned his own printing service, Web Press Tension, Inc. Paul had helped many vets before us, but we were especially amazed at the extent of his sacrifice in our case—he'd come all the way from Colonia, New Jersey, to find us.

Paul was generous to the Spirit of America, and he walked with us a while, entertaining us with his jokes and his harmonica. He played "Anchors Aweigh," the Marine Corps anthem, and many popular tunes. "Why don't you accompany Sing-Along here?" I asked.

Marshall interrupted, with opinions of his own. "Bob, I sing a cappella, you know that!"

There in Indianapolis, we didn't have any idea that Paul would appear again and again during the rest of our trip. Always with a joke. Always eager to lift our spirits.

As we walked through Indianapolis we stayed with Barbara

and Darryl Tomey, out in the country in Fillmore. Darryl was a well driller. What gracious, kind people they were, even going the extra mile of planning a surprise forty-first birthday party for me.

The set-up was like this: our new friend Paul Beutell asked me go with him to a Veterans of Foreign Wars meeting in Indianapolis. Marshall had told him, "Be sure you have him back for this surprise birthday party. He doesn't have a hint."

Wouldn't you know, we were delayed about two or three hours. A lot of work went into that party, and in spite of my delay, I had a wonderful celebration for another year of my life.

My trampoline had become a vital part of my fitness routine. I would frequently stop and Marshall would take out the trampoline. I'd stand on my head, then roll onto my back, and bounce up and down. A crowd often gathered at this point and people would ask what I was doing and why. The reason was simple. Fatigued muscles build up excess levels of lactic acid. Standing on my head served to get my blood flowing and revitalize me. Then I'd sit on the trampoline and relax awhile, visiting with the people who stopped to watch me.

Many of the people who stopped wanted to encourage us. To some, I was a curiosity. I understood their attitude, since I knew I didn't have my sights on an everyday, run-of-the-mill goal. A number of people who stopped were Vietnam vets, eager to greet us and offer their help.

We had decided to walk Route 40 instead of the nearby interstate, figuring we'd run into less traffic. But as we came into Richmond, we ran into road construction. Highway workers were paving "old 40," and they had closed the outside lane. This didn't bother me. But Marshall . . .

All the construction made him restless, so he decided to go off for a ride on his bicycle.

I didn't see it happen. He was behind me. But because the outside lane was barricaded, a driver didn't stop at a stop sign. He pulled out of a side road, right into Marshall's path. Marshall had two choices. He could hit the brakes to avoid a collision, or he could make a quick right turn up the side road.

He opted for the latter. It might have worked, if he hadn't hit some gravel, which threw both wheels out from under him. Witnesses said he moved like a stunt man in the movies— flying six feet up in the air before landing in a prone position.

When I looked back to see what was happening, I was horrified as I thought he had hit his head. I started moving toward him as fast as I could.

Marshall is not the kind of guy who gives up easily. He tried to get up. I'm not sure who called the ambulance, but one arrived within a few minutes.

Marshall had dislocated his shoulder. The emergency-room doctor decided to bring in an orthopedic surgeon and it was four hours before Marshall's shoulder could be popped back into place. That was one long, painful wait—for both of us.

When Marshall was finally released, he was given strict orders to keep his arm in a sling. He left the hospital with it on, and he even arrived at our guest quarters that day, Yoke Fellows Institute in Cambridge, with the sling. But that was the last time I saw it. He put it away and the next day was back on the job. Despite his pain, he was there for me. He could still drive the car, and he was able to pull out the trampoline, double up the wheelchair, and carry on. He just started swinging that arm, to exercise it and loosen it up. I prayed for my friend, and the shoulder healed beautifully. I did take Mark 16:18 to heart: "They will place their hands on sick people, and they will get well."

Before we left Indiana, we stayed with a widow, who lived in a large white wooden-frame house that Marshall and I called "Cat Heaven Hotel." Marshall seemed to attract cats, and the widow's dozen cats took an immediate liking to him. The minute he sat down, the fur began to fly—cat squabbles over who would sit in his lap.

The lady of the house, Mrs. Parsons, was delighted with this scene, saying, "See, cats are a good judge of character."

I said, "I've always said Marshall was a character." By this time a tabby was trying to clean Marshall's face, while another jet black cat with kittens was trying to climb up his pants leg.

"Where did you get all these cats?" I asked, as we sat in her living room.

"Oh, here and there. Many of them show up at the back door and I adopt them. I used to have more, thirty."

"Thirty!" Marshall and I said in unison.

Marshall, who believed that cats should be seen and not heard—and kept outside—was trying to get one orange Morris-type cat off his lap. The cat, big enough for three normal cats, refused to budge. He purred so loudly he sounded like a motor boat getting revved up.

"Isn't that cute?" said Mrs. Parsons as she served us tea. "Robespierre really loves you, Marshall. Why, I never before saw him take up like this with a stranger."

Marshall smiled as he tried to balance his china tea cup and his plate of cookies while Robespierre still purred loudly on his lap.

From behind the couch the black cat attacked Robespierre, sticking his paw in the tea cup and upsetting the hot tea, all over Marshall and the Victorian couch.

Marshall jumped up, bodily removed the orange cat, and moved to a wing-back chair near the fireplace. He had hardly started his second cup of tea before Robespierre jumped into his lap again, purring even louder.

That night I laughed all the way to bed. If cats are a good judge of character, Marshall must be one of the best men alive. He was sure at the top of Robespierre's list.

While we finished our Indiana leg and began the Ohio leg of our trek, we stayed with Carmen and Don Smith and their daughter, Tara, in Pinkerton, Ohio. Don loaned Marshall his old pickup truck so we could haul our trailer to Dayton. Unfortunately, the ball on the back of the truck wasn't the right size, and Marshall couldn't lock it securely. Still, he thought it would work.

As Marshall and I were pulling the trailer down the highway on a foggy, rainy morning, we approached a bridge. Our tire hit a concrete lip, and the trailer snapped loose. The trailer was now a free-moving vehicle, going about 45 m.p.h. over a freeway bridge, with traffic not far behind it. I prayed.

As the trailer continued over the bridge, it sideswiped the concrete restraining wall, rolled over a small fence, and came to a stop on an inside lane of the bridge. It all occurred so fast, I hardly knew what had happened.

As we stood there looking at the somewhat battered trailer, I realized how serious this mishap might have been. If it had snapped loose anywhere else than on the bridge, it could have careened into the oncoming lane of traffic. But God was looking out for us, and Marshall learned a valuable lesson about presumptuous faith. Even though the Holy Spirit protects us, that doesn't relieve us of the responsibility of checking things out before hand.

Near the border Marshall and I were also sobered at what we saw and heard at a high school where I spoke to a group of athletes, mostly weight lifters and football players. Outside the gym I saw a group of kids popping pills, and I could smell marijuana. I said to Marshall, "These kids don't know what trouble they're inviting in."

Then as we walked into the gym I felt a lot of tension in the air. Some of the guys were flexing and heavy competition was obviously the name of the game. One of the guys, a senior, looked like a young version of Arnold Schwarzenegger.

While waiting to be introduced, I listened to a former body-building champion talk about his training program, which included the systematic use of steroids. He gave the students quite a show. To music he flexed each major muscle group. His body shone with oil. He did a weight-lifting demonstration, asking one of the kids to spot him. He really believed in himself.

I looked around and could see that the kids were impressed, almost mesmerized. A question and answer period followed. "What do you eat?" someone asked. He gave a list of vitamins, some of which I'd never heard of.

"No, what kind of food do you eat?"

"High carbs. Fish, chicken, broiled or baked. Plenty of complex carbs. And eight to twelve glasses of water."

"How did you get your size?"

The coach and teachers watched carefully, somewhat

suspicious, I thought. He answered, "Hard work. Hard work, man. Real hard work."

Another kid asked, "Well, we still want to know—how did you get your size?"

Just as the bodybuilder started to answer, one of the coaches mentioned that his time was up; the kids could ask more questions after the meeting. The muscle man received a standing ovation as he left the platform.

I was then introduced as a world-class power-lifting champion. As I prepared to do my first lift, I briefly gave my testimony. At first I had difficulty bench pressing 375 pounds. I had walked all day, and it had taken its toll. Finally, I made a clean lift and everyone applauded. I followed my lift with a two-finger planche (push-up done without your feet on the ground). That got the kids excited. "That-a-way to go, Bob," a bunch of kids shouted. After I completed my testimony, I took their questions.

How long did I work out? How many times a week did I work out? What did I eat? How did I get my size?

"Preparation," I said. "I believe in preparation. That means I also keep a notebook of my progress; I rely on a power higher than myself. I also believe in setting and working toward goals."

"Hey, man, but how did you get your size? 'Roids, you took 'roids, right?"

"Wrong!" I exploded. "I have never taken any kind of steroid or drug. Steroids are not necessary. In fact, they can kill you."

The bodybuilder, who was watching, piped up, "Hey, every real athlete uses steroids at one time or another. You're still living in the Dark Ages, man."

"That's not true," I said emphatically. "I know many who don't. There are more athletes who don't use drugs than who do."

My time was up and I thanked the coaches and student body before leaving the platform. I prayed that at least one kid had heard me.

Immediately, the bodybuilder challenged me to a public weight-lifting competition. It was as if he were asking for a contest between steroid strength and human strength—although he didn't realize that I didn't rely on human strength; I always asked God to anoint me with His strength.

Marshall said, "Bob, you've got to be tired. Don't do it. It's a game."

But after saying a silent prayer I felt I should accept the challenge.

The champion bodybuilder was in great shape, and I trusted that I wasn't acting out of presumptuous faith. "You go first," he said, and I got up on the bench. In preparation, I began to pray silently. I knew my energy level was low, but almost immediately I could feel the power of the Holy Spirit rise up in me like on that afternoon I did my best lift ever—breaking my record at the United States Powerlifting Championships meet in Santa Monica. The kids went crazy, and I jumped down, praising God all the way.

Then it was the weight lifter's turn. He got up, confident of his artificial steroid power. I felt badly for him when he almost dropped the weights on top of himself. He just couldn't get it together. Finally, he gave up and left in a hurry.

Marshall and I stayed a while longer, explaining to the kids the difference between a supernatural high and a steroid-built false energy which leads to physical damage and sometimes even death.

When we finally left I was sure we had made a lasting impression on some of the kids and teachers.

"Everybody does it" isn't true. There's a better way than drugs.

16

OHIO: HERE COME THE VETS

Our Ohio walk started off with two big surprises. First, the bad news: Ohio law said we couldn't walk the interstate.

The good news: No sooner had I crossed over into Ohio than I was surprised with a grand welcoming party. The drivers of five or six semis, in single file, laid on a symphony of air horns for about five minutes. At the same time a group of veterans dressed in fatigues, including Paul Beutell, came marching by, carrying their rifles. About seventy-five Vietnam veterans came out and the drill sergeant among them said, "Fall in." They all jumped into that column, heads high and shoulders back.

In one sense, it was a hilarious scene. You never saw so many pot bellies stuffed into uniforms that didn't fit! One sergeant with a real low voice was especially touching. He enjoyed barking out those march commands. The men asked me to lead the parade and I did. I believe we could have made it to Washington, D.C., that night had we kept walking, because we were feeling so high on patriotic spirit. Looking straight ahead, we marched about a mile together before breaking up.

The truckers pulled into a truck stop at the state border, and they laid on their horns again for what seemed like forever. Then the governor sent his officials over to say that they would try to cut through the red tape and bureaucracy so we could walk on the highway. Although, right then, that didn't seem as important to me as did the loyalty, support, and camaraderie I felt from the vets.

Suddenly, I realized that the Spirit of America movement was gaining momentum for its final push toward Washington. Throughout Ohio, vets from Vietnam, Korea, and even World War II had showed up in force to help us on our way. Word had gotten out and the spirit had caught on.

When we'd returned from Nam, veterans had received much undeserved, bad publicity. Where was the press now to cover the attempts of veterans to feed the needy of our country? As I walked through Ohio, vets from all over the state mobilized to collect and distribute food in their areas. Marshall and I were grateful for the help we received—both from veterans' organizations and individual veterans who walked with us or donated money.

Actually, the Ohio state government was the first to give us an official escort. Since Route 40 was more dangerous than some highways, due to its lack of paved shoulder, we went right to the top and asked the people we knew in the governor's office for help. Almost immediately the state provided a yellow truck, with two drivers, that rode behind us through part of the state. We were grateful for the help.

Still followed by the yellow state truck, Marshall and I had the opportunity to visit a veterans' hospital outside of Dayton. Veterans from three wars gathered to hear me speak.

Before my talk, we visited the wards that housed the mentally ill and the severe alcoholics. I felt so much compassion, seeing the effects the constant stress and traumatic memories had left on the soldiers. One red-haired man thought he was an aggressive gorilla, leaping toward another man who thought he was Superman. One black man, singing in a monotone sing-song voice, stared into space. A slender man, convinced he was an eagle, claimed he could fly, if he only had a ledge to jump off of to prove it. Another man had smoked so much pot and drunk so much alcohol that he had obviously damaged his brain. One moment he would chirp like a bird; the next, he would croak like a frog. I felt so helpless, trying to communicate with those who were so far out of touch with reality.

I felt that many of these men were possessed with demons, and from my understanding of nutrition I knew that most of these veterans were in a toxic condition. There wasn't much that Marshall and I could do, except pray for their salvation, healing, and deliverance.

We were heartily welcomed by the other soldiers who had been injured in or were ill as a result of the Vietnam war. They were an attentive audience; we had so much in common.

After my talk, Marshall and I agreed that we would spend extra time, greeting each man individually. In one of the wards I noticed one soldier lying very still. I went over to his bed and said, "Hey, man, how's it going?"

"Not too cool," he answered, nearly in a whisper.

It was a sunny day. I tried to encourage him, get him to look on the bright side of life.

"The birds are still singing," I said.

"I wouldn't know," he mumbled.

The conversation was getting nowhere. He seemed so down.

"Why are you so happy?" he finally asked. "Your legs are gone and they aren't ever coming back."

"Do you believe in miracles?" I asked.

"No, I don't, and how could you believe? You're maimed for life." It seemed he was getting agitated, even angry with me.

"I do, would you like to know why?"

He turned his face away from me, toward the wall.

"Would you like to know why I believe?" I asked again.

The gaunt soldier seemed to ignore my question. I wanted so much to reach him. I prayed silently, searching for an open door to witness.

He said, "What are you, a fool or something?"

"If I am a fool," I said, "I'm a fool for Jesus."

"It's too late for me to hear about Jesus," he exploded. "I'm dying. Yeh, I'm dying." He began to weep openly, as if his heart were broken.

At first I was at a loss for words. Then I asked him to turn around so I could see his face. As he turned around, I told him all I knew about Jesus: that Jesus had died for him so that he could live and have eternal life. "If you died tonight," I asked him, "do you know where you'd go?"

He didn't know for sure.

I invited him to say the sinner's prayer with me and ask Jesus into his life. I waited through a long silence. Finally he said he'd think about it. We prayed, and I thanked God that I had felt led to stop and talk to this spiritually hungry man.

As Christmas 1985 drew near, I felt particularly homesick. I was longing to get home to spend the holiday with Jackey and our family. I had flight reservations and knew I'd get there, but the cold days dragged on.

One December afternoon as we drove down the road, I saw a scraggly evergreen tree, so weather-beaten that it was hanging on by its roots for dear life. Right past the tree was parked a large dilapidated station wagon. Inside we could see a man, woman, and some small children.

I said, "Why don't we stop and see if they need help." Marshall was agreeable.

Upon closer investigation, the family of five was dressed in tattered clothing. None of them wore a coat. They had run out of gas. They were out of money and out of food. The mother cradled a baby that cried a sickly cry, then coughed. "Hey, mister, what are you doing out here?" the man asked me.

I gave my standard introduction. "My name is Bob Wieland and this is Marshall Cardiff. We're walking across America to feed spiritually and physically hungry people."

The woman looked at us quizzically, as if to say, *Are you for real?*

The man spoke. "I'm Joseph Peterson, and this is my wife, Carrie. As you can see, we're stranded out here, and my wife and kids are awfully hungry."

I looked at the children. They reminded me of the emaciated orphans in Vietnam. "What are your names?" I asked.

"Cherry," said the girl.

"Paul," said the boy.

Marshall had already headed for our food supply. Joe

continued, "I don't want something for nothing. I'm a hard worker. What I really need is a job.

His wife piped up, "He is a hard worker."

Marshall and I held a conference at the side of the road, then I returned to the station wagon. "Marshall tells me we need things straightened out in our trailer. We didn't have time to find help in town."

His eyes lit up. "Well, I'm real good at putting things in order, aren't I, honey?"

"Yes, he really is," she said.

"We can afford to pay you $50.00 and give you some gas to get into town. We know of a shelter where you can stay till you get work."

Joe shook my hand and then Marshall's. "It's a deal," he said, standing a little taller.

His wife began to cry and then the kids chimed in to make a chorus of it. Before Joe started to work, we invited them to join us for a late lunch, which they wolfed down.

Marshall and I slipped an envelope of extra cash to Carrie when Joe wasn't looking. "Here, this is for the kids for Christmas," I said. The spirit of Christmas brightened up for me that afternoon as I reached out to help this couple. We filled up their tank with our extra gas and helped start the car.

From that day on, I got "into" the Christmas spirit, even going Christmas caroling near our host's home in Hebron, Ohio, and decorating the Mason family tree.

Before I knew it, I was airborne, heading for southern California, where I would enjoy the "home fires" until after the New Year. A green Christmas was just fine by me. I appreciated being able to rest awhile and enjoy Jackey's open arms.

Actually, many doctors and physical therapists considered my gait and mileage a physical impossibility. To complete the trip at all I knew I would have to rest appropriately and care for my body—just as I always had. Of course, I also wanted to keep my marriage strong, but these rest periods were essential, just to keep going.

After the holidays, Marshall and I picked up where we'd left off, at Zanesville, Ohio. We were rested and looking forward to spring, though Washington was still a long way off.

Marshall still broke up the monotony of some of his days by going off on side trips to see the sights. In Ohio he explored caverns, including Olentangy Caverns, the only three-level caves in Ohio, and the Seneca Caverns, discovered in 1872, Marshall reported, when a hunting dog chased a rabbit into a pit. The dog didn't return, but two boys could hear her barking under the ground. As they dug, the limestone collapsed and they tumbled about twelve feet into a cave. It sounded like Alice in Wonderland.

Now Marshall really got going. "What fascinates me, Bob, is that Seneca Caverns weren't formed by erosion, but by a fracture in the limestone bedrock."

I knew Marshall was going to hit me with a new geological question, so I said, "No diastrophism, Marshall?"

"Hey, Bob, you're catching on!"

Late one afternoon, Marshall and I began to recount our blessings. Once we'd left New Mexico, we'd stayed in a chain of homes all the way across the U.S.A. For the most part, we saw a common thread through the seventy-three homes we had stayed in. The same loving, caring spirit that existed in my childhood home was still alive in many places. The American people were exceptionally kind, opening their homes and hearts to us. Many even gave money. According to Scripture, we knew that the prayer and good works that these people extended on our behalf would not return to them void.

Marshall got the brunt of the work on those days that we moved from one home to another. He would load the motorcycle on the little trailer behind the van. Then he'd load up all our gear and bags. We'd jump in the front and he'd take me to the place where I'd stopped walking the night before. We'd pray, then I'd get started.

While I walked, Marshall would move all our stuff to the next home and take the motorcycle off the trailer. Then he'd come back and check on me and then he'd go back to the house we were moving out of and bring his bicycle and trailer and the igloo and the cold water and come back up to me. And that's the way we inched across America.

In Chandlersville we stayed with Joe Long and his wife, Ruth, an attractive woman with a sweet spirit. Brown-haired, stocky Joe, a road worker, was laid off during that winter, so he decided to walk with us for a month.

I could see right away that Joe had witnessing potential, but he admitted that he sometimes felt shy. Verbal witness was a challenge for him. So Marshall and I decided to work on Joe's confidence.

"Joe," I said, "sometimes it's difficult to witness, but we have to remember that the Holy Spirit guides us and gives us the words to say. When I feel the Spirit nudge me, that's when I move. Sometimes Marshall just plants seeds; sometimes it's just not the right time."

"How do you know when it's the right time?" asked Joe.

"You just feel it in your gut. Why, just today, you ministered with us out here, and a number of people were saved." This had happened day after day: Joe came out and walked with us and people got saved. Joe's confidence and courage and effectiveness multiplied steadily over the month, all the way to Wheeling, West Virginia, a hundred miles from his home near Zanesville. He'd go home every night and drive back out to where I'd be the following day.

Eventually Joe joined us only on Saturdays, when he'd bring friends with him, who would bring popcorn, knowing how much I enjoyed it. It was amazing, Joe never knew exactly where we'd be on a Saturday, but he always found us. We had a great time witnessing and enjoying one another's company. Seeing Joe's commitment to serve the Lord and knowing the effort he put forth to make our journey comfortable really touched my heart.

People like Joe Long helped me to realize that I had made the right choice when I'd followed God's direction to go out and walk the highways and share the gospel. I could see the kingdom of God expanding as I encouraged others like Joe to do likewise.

As we neared the West Virginia border, a semi stopped. The driver admitted that he'd been watching me all the way across the country, for two-and-a-half years. He'd always drive by, tooting his horn and waving. So many truckers honked that I didn't recognize his truck. Apparently, he had passed me every two weeks or so. But finally, this day, under conviction of the Holy Spirit, he stopped and invited Jesus Christ into his life.

In his wanderings, Marshall had discovered that the Ohio state motto is "With God all things are possible." Of course it's a Bible verse—but more recently the words have been put to music. On the road Marshall loved to sing that song. It became our theme song: "With God all things are possible."

The writers of the Gospels knew it. The pioneers of Ohio knew it. Marshall and I knew it. Believe me, you can know it too.

17

WEST VIRGINIA, PENNSYLVANIA, AND MARYLAND: PLANTING SEEDS, HARVESTING SOULS

The hills of West Virginia look like an oversized, gentle roller coaster. One West Virginian sticks out in my mind. One day from out of the soft green-dressed hills, walked a skinny, bearded mountain man, carrying a jug. "Howdy," he said. "Where you from?"

"California," I said.

He took a swig of corn liquor and asked, "What you doin' in these parts?"

"We're walking to Washington, D.C."

Without a pause he said, "No doubt in my mind, you're gonna make it. How long you reckon it's gonna take?"

"Hard to tell. We just keep on walking," we replied.

"Well, let me tell you. There's no doubt in my mind, you're gonna make it," he said, swigging from the bottle.

We thanked him and decided to move on, since the conversation, at least on his end, had reduced itself: "There's no doubt in my mind, you're gonna make it."

As we walked, Marshall joked that any doubts he'd had about our success had just vanished. It was obvious, if this West Virginian was telling the truth, we were "gonna make it."

For the most part, Marshall and I found that Americans are kind and generous to strangers. Many of the people we stayed with treated us like family. A West Virginian named Fred, with whom we stayed for a few days, was no exception, although we soon learned that he had one small failing that overshadowed the rest of his life.

Fred was a retired accountant crippled with osteoarthritis. He was a small man, so bent with age that he needed a cane to get around. He paid his retired neighbor, a woman named Pat Clawson, to cook his meals and clean his small two-bedroom wooden-frame home.

Fred was lonely and told us about his wife of forty years, who had died suddenly of a stroke several years before. "I'm sorry to hear that," Marshall said. "My wife's gone too."

One morning, Pat Clawson told me, "Fred Sr. doesn't need to be so lonely. He has a son, Fred Jr., who wants to visit in the worst way."

Marshall asked, "Well, why doesn't he?"

"Because Fred Jr. made the mistake of marrying a pretty young black school teacher," Pat said. "Fred Sr. couldn't accept it. When his son wanted to bring her home for dinner, Fred Sr. refused to see them or allow them in the house. One night I overheard Fred Sr. call his son on the phone. The son's wife must have answered because the old man said, 'This is Mr. Henry. Is my son at home?' Can you imagine how she must have felt? Why, it's almost like she didn't exist."

"Perhaps in his mind she *didn't* exist," Marshall said.

What a senseless tragedy, especially when Fred Sr. seemed so lonely.

Soon we entered Pennsylvania, where vets came out in droves to meet and greet us. Again, Paul Beutell was there with a smile— and a mysterious hint of a surprise waiting for us in D.C. "Just wait and see," he said with a glint in his eye. "Just wait and see." Fortunately (or unfortunately, depending on how you looked at it) Paul had picked up a whole new repertoire of corny jokes. His sense of humor really livened up our days.

Someone along the way compared Marshall and me to Johnny Appleseed, sowing the Word of God, instead of apple seeds. We expected a harvest of people who loved God and would help put America back together again. And on this last leg of our journey, we saw some immediate results of our seed planting.

In Pittsburgh, Marshall and I were scheduled to visit another veterans' hospital. The long corridors reminded me of my Philadelphia days, gurney racing Ed Henry down the halls. This Pittsburgh hospital was spotless. The grounds and buildings looked well cared for. And so did the veterans.

As we walked through the wards, paying respect to these men and women who had laid their futures on the line, I once again felt so grateful that my life had been spared. More than ever, I appreciated the training my parents had provided when I was a child. Their years of love and encouragement had helped me maintain the positive attitude that had kept me going in the hospital. I looked around at the veterans, of all ages, from all backgrounds. Some of them would never go home from this place.

In a ward of elderly patients, a blind veteran called out for a glass of water.

I poured some into a glass and handed it to him.

"Where you from?" we both asked at the same time.

"Wisconsin," he said, "Madison, Wisconsin."

"Hey, I'm originally from Milwaukee."

"Well, what do you know?" he said. "We're both native sons. My name's George Lewis." He reached out his hand, which trembled as I shook it.

George, I found out, had been paralyzed from the waist down and blinded by an explosion of nerve gas. Since World War II, for most of his life, he'd been confined to one hospital after another. He was so frail, not more than eighty-five pounds. His silver hair was so thin I could see his shiny scalp. And yet he had an air of peace about him.

I briefly shared my story with George.

"You know," he responded, "I'm getting ready to die."

Heavy, I thought. *Why is he telling me this? Lord, how do you want me to answer?* I said, "You know, George, I don't look at physical death. As I see it, when that day comes, I'm just going to check into a new hotel, a hotel named heaven."

His voice was getting weaker; the conversation was tiring him out. "My doctors told me I have cancer. It's spread through my body, and I could go anytime," he said as if he were resigned to dying.

"George, I'd like to tell you about Jesus Christ, my Lord, my Comforter. Do you know Him?"

"I did know Him as a child, but it's been a long time. I guess I'd forgotten about Him."

"Well, did you accept Jesus as your Lord and Savior way back then?"

"I think I did; I don't remember."

Just then Marshall walked in, reminding me that it was time to give our talk in the main lounge.

But before I left, I invited George, for heavenly insurance's sake, to repeat the sinner's prayer as the three of us held hands.

George's voice was failing, but he managed to make it to the amen. "George," I said, "it's time for Marshall and me to go. But this isn't good-bye. I know we'll see you again, in heaven with Jesus!"

As we started to walk out, a nurse came in. In passing she said, "We don't know what's keeping him alive. By all reports he should have been dead a long time ago." Marshall and I exchanged glances. God had his reasons, we silently agreed.

My testimony was well received and the day proceeded according to plan. We continued to visit the wards and talk to the men until dusk, when we finally got ready to leave.

"Let's stop by to say good-bye to George," I said.

"Sure," answered Marshall, but when we got there the bed was empty.

George had died in his sleep soon after we'd left his room.

In downtown Pittsburgh the vets had set up huge Spirit of America containers in which passersby could drop food. As we prepared to go out on one of the food drives, Marshall and I remarked how well adjusted so many of these vets seemed. The media presented a distorted picture of the average Vietnam vet, as living in the past, loudly complaining about a long list of ailments, and suffering from post-traumatic stress. If these men in Pennsylvania, who took time to donate their services to the Spirit of America, were like vets across the country, I felt proud to be counted in their company. They showed a giving and caring spirit, even to the homeless people. The vets treated them with respect and dignity—like equals.

Of course there were and are vets who haven't been able to cope with the effects of the war. I remembered the men in the veterans' hospitals. And here in Pittsburgh I counseled with friends of a vet who'd been taken to a mental institution. Waking from a war nightmare, he'd mistaken his wife for the enemy and tried to strangle her. But that was the exception, not the rule.

Sandy, the leader of one veterans' group, remarked, "Hey Bob, how come you seem so centered, so peaceful?"

I immediately borrowed Marshall's Bible. Before I actually said anything, Sandy wanted to know what the Bible had to do with life here and now. Knowing an open door, I said, "The living Word in this Bible is part of my peace; Jesus is my peace," I replied.

Perplexed, he looked at me, scratched his head, then quickly changed the subject. He suddenly remembered he had an appointment and disappeared.

"That's okay," I said to Marshall. "We planted more seeds. It was better to have tried to witness than not to have tried at all."

Marshall patted my shoulder. "That's right," he said. Right there we stopped and prayed that God would send people to bring Sandy to the Lord.

Before we left Pittsburgh, Marshall and I were grand marshals in a parade organized to honor the Spirit of America. Again, the vets showed up in large numbers, and the true spirit of America welled up within the marchers.

At the end of the parade we spotted Sandy, who felt the Lord had touched him in a special way. Here in Pennsylvania God was doing a special work, drawing military men into His own army.

Uniontown, Pennsylvania, also put out the red carpet for us, even giving us the key to the city in a special ceremony. The people of Uniontown organized a Spirit of America parade.

Being a grand marshal was something I could learn to live with. Again, generations of veterans came out to help us collect and distribute food for the hungry—and blankets for the homeless.

Marshall discovered that there were over one hundred state parks in Pennsylvania, much loved by its natives. Marshall admitted that, if he had the time, he'd visit every one of them. But we walked only a corner of Pennsylvania, heading down toward the Maryland border, south of Pittsburgh.

All the way through Maryland we saw signs: "George Washington slept here." That man was either very sleepy—or there was more than one of him!

Marshall joked, "Now, Bob, do you think we'll go down in the history books: Bob Wieland and Marshall Cardiff slept here?"

As we came down out of the mountains, into the rolling hills, which eventually flattened out along the east coast, I felt almost as if I were coasting.

Near Baltimore an older man, driving slowly down the road in a well-preserved Model T, stopped to talk. Peering over his glasses, he said, "Mister, what are you doing here?"

I started my standard introduction. "My friend Marshall Cardiff and I are walking across the United States to feed spiritually and physically hungry people."

"You know, mister," he said sympathetically, "there must be a much easier way to raise money. . . . You look *real* tired!"

Though I was physically tired that day, my spirits were high because I was close to my goal. "I'm sure there might be an easier way to raise money," I said, "but I'm just as interested in raising people's awareness to the needs of hungry people. And it's working. Since we've been walking and getting media coverage, *We Are the World* has raised millions of dollars. So you see, we feel we are accomplishing exactly what we set out to do. Right, Marshall?"

"Right, Bob," Marshall replied enthusiastically.

"Would you care to make a contribution and sponsor some steps? Your contribution is tax deductible," Marshall invited.

"No, I don't think so," said the man. "You know, mister, the government has programs to feed the hungry and the home-less. It's not our job."

"I don't agree, sir," I said. "Many of us have extra money, food and clothing to share with those less fortunate than ourselves. We are known abroad as the most wasteful nation in the world. There's no reason I can think of that we shouldn't help our government help others by giving our surplus. By the way, sir, my name is Bob Wieland. What's yours?"

"Hymie Levy," he answered begrudgingly.

"Mr. Levy," I began.

"You can call me Hymie, or Hy for short."

"Hy, Marshall and I feel that the main purpose of our trip is to witness and minister to America's spiritually hungry, to tell them about the unconditional love of the Lord Jesus Christ."

Then Marshall briefly explained about the life of Jesus, His purpose, and how my accepting Him as Lord and Savior had enabled me to accomplish what God had given me to do.

"Is there any reason why you wouldn't want to receive Jesus as your own personal Lord and Savior?" I asked.

Hy paused a minute before answering. "I'm not a man who makes fast decisions. I'd like to think about it. Do you have any literature?"

He acted as if we were trying to sell him a car; he wanted to check out his options.

"Sure," said Marshall, "here's a brochure."

"Say, Bob," Hy turned to me, "I like you, but I think you should turn back before you get hit by a car or truck or someone beats you up or kills you and dumps you by the side of the road."

Marshall remarked, "That's what I call positive thinking!"

We thanked Hy for stopping and continued on walking.

His last words were, "Don't blame me if something happens to you. I warned you!"

I prayed for him for a couple of days.

Several days later, wouldn't you know it, Hy pulled up beside us. He was smiling as he got out of the car.

"Bob," he said, "the night after I left you, right after I read your brochure, I had a dream. I swear, a man who said He was Jesus and an angel appeared. He didn't say anything, just held

His arms outstretched toward me. The next day a neighbor gave me a birthday present. It was a picture of Jesus standing at a door with no handle. Waiting for someone to open it from the inside. Sonny," he continued, "I'm ready to accept Jesus as my Savior. The Lord Jesus was a Jew like me, you know."

Marshall and I embraced him, and we said the sinner's prayer with him. "Welcome home, Hy," Marshall and I said in unison.

He was crying unashamedly, tears of joy.

This time when we said good-bye, his last words were, "Say, do you have any more of those brochures? I'd like to give some to my family."

We gave him a bundle and walked on toward D.C., praising the Lord.

18

WALL TWENTY-TWO WEST, LINE FORTY-SEVEN: WASHINGTON, D.C.

Marshall and I began every day by reading Ephesians 6:12: "Our struggle is not against flesh and blood, but against the rulers, against the authorities, against the powers of this dark world and against the spiritual forces of evil in the heavenly realms." The closer we got to our finish line, the more confidently we claimed victory in Jesus Christ. Although at times I felt physically exhausted, a sense of God's overwhelming power and joy rose up within me, higher and higher as we approached the last mile.

My goal was the Vietnam Memorial, the black marble wall erected to the memory of my comrades who had fallen in battle. The war had cut short their lives and had drastically changed the course of my life. It seemed only appropriate that my journey should end there.

Marshall had already made arrangements. Our plan called for me to walk within one mile of the wall and then quit, saving that last mile for midday, May 14, 1986.

The day before, with only that last mile remaining, Marshall and I drove to the Washington Airport, anticipating a grand reunion. Lieutenant Jim Sylvester, whom I hadn't seen in sixteen years, was flying in for the event. I also looked forward to seeing David Denier and Dennis Cooper.

I recognized Lieutenant Sylvester as soon as he got off the plane. His first words were, "You look a lot better than the last time I saw you!" Lieutenant Sylvester, along with Dennis, had been one of the last guys to see me before the accident. Jim had actually seen me get hit. When out on patrol as a medic I had always stayed close to Jim and Hopkins, the radio man.

"It's great to see you." said Jim as we hugged each other.

My parents flew in, as did Margaret Harvey, my secretary. Jackey chose to stay home, since Marshall and I had made plans to leave for Canada immediately after we completed the journey. Jackey and I decided we would celebrate the victory privately when I got home. I had felt her love and support every step of the way, and I could feel it on that last mile—as if she were at my side.

Others came from around the country, including Harry Sneider, my training associate; the Philips family from Missouri; Joe and Ruth Long and their daughters; and Paul Beutell; and many, many more.

The night before the final mile, everybody got together for a walk reunion. What a great time! These people and more, including Dr. Ash Hayes, executive director of the President's Council on Physical Fitness, and George Otott, with Life Cycle and Life Gyms, would walk behind me those final steps of the journey. Tony Diamond, a Vietnam vet from Southern California, had joined us to videotape the event. To see the vision finally fulfilled was so reassuring—because God had completed that which He had said was going to be done.

The next morning, before starting out, there was a surprise for me. I had a ten o'clock appointment at the White House! That was the surprise that Paul and Catherine Buetell had hinted at. I was thankful for their efforts, and for those of Congressman Smith of New Jersey, who actually arranged the meeting.

So at ten o'clock, Marshall, Margaret, and I headed for the Oval Office. Right outside the gate of the White House, a man wearing a Spirit of America hat came up to us. I'd seen him before, but . . .

"Do you know where we met him?" I whispered to Marshall,

who was always good at filling me in on information. "Was it Cumberland, Maryland?" Marshall didn't remember.

The man held out his hand and said exuberantly, "Hey, Bob, I've been here since six this morning, waiting for you." His name was on the tip of my tongue. But I'd met thousands of people and just couldn't figure out who this was.

He continued, "Yeh, I wouldn't have missed this day for anything. Flew all night to get here."

Then it dawned on me. It was Dana Braker, a man who had helped Tom and me all the way back in Casa Grande, Arizona! He'd traveled across the entire country, even though he hadn't seen me in two-and-a-half years.

We talked for a few minutes, but then I had to excuse myself—I didn't want to keep the President waiting. Years before, at the dedication of the Vietnam wall, I had wished that I could someday have a personal conversation with President Reagan. Now, as we were ushered into the Oval Office, that dream was coming true.

There, right before my eyes, was Ronald Reagan, the President of the United States, looking cordial and glad to see us. Marshall and Margaret stood silently by my side. For a few moments, we were tongue-tied.

The President approached me and shook my hand. He had a warm firm handshake, and his smile made us feel at home immediately. Recovering my composure, I presented him with a Spirit of America T-shirt, which he graciously accepted.

I said, "I'm very happy to be able to meet you." Then he chatted with us and gave us some mementos of our visit to the Oval Office.

Then the President asked me where I got the strength to complete my journey. I just said, "I'm just an ordinary guy with a supernatural Father—God is the source of my strength."

The President nodded, and I suspected he knew what I was talking about. Our conversation lasted fifteen or twenty minutes. Then we left the White House—ready to walk the last mile to the wall.

The press was out in force. I appreciated the publicity in behalf of our walk for physical and spiritual hunger, though I sensed the reporters were thinking of a story along the lines of "Handicapped Boy Crawls Across America." Another fact struck me: I didn't recognize any of the reporters. They hadn't covered my walk before now; they were just here for the finale. No matter how tired I was, I wanted to surprise these guys, give them a run for their money!

Marshall and I started that last mile with prayer, just as we had started every day. Then I took off as fast as I could. The press, walking beside me nonchalantly with their cameras, woke up fast. They thought maybe I could keep this "over-drive" up for five or ten minutes, but I think we covered the last mile in forty minutes—about twice my normal pace. All of a sudden everybody realized that what I was doing was for real.

My support team marched behind me. Even though I couldn't see them, I could feel their love and support surrounding me. Dennis, Dave, and Jim Sylvester carried a United States flag up the tree-lined streets. My mom and dad were also right behind me.

Each step I took, I could feel God's supernatural energy flowing around me and in me, and my speed picked up like never before. One step at a time, slowly and steadily, I finally reached the long black expanse of the Vietnam Memorial.

I yanked off my "shoes" and raised my hands in victory. We had proved that "nothing is impossible with God."

Bob in a promotional photo—athlete and hero

Bob at a relief camp in Dacca, Bangladesh

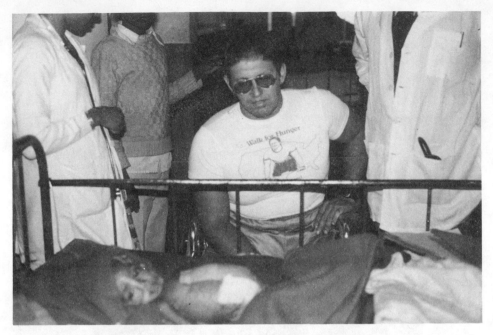

Bob making a visit in a Dacca hospital; world hunger cannot be ignored

Bob shakes hands with another victim of war

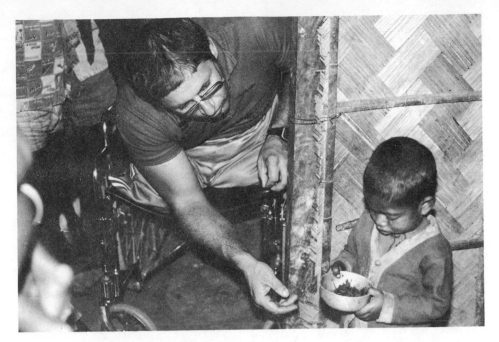

Making a Bengali friend

Entertaining his new friends in Dacca with his inimitable planche

Bob on his custom-designed marathon bike, with his coach of eleven years, Dr. Harry Sneider

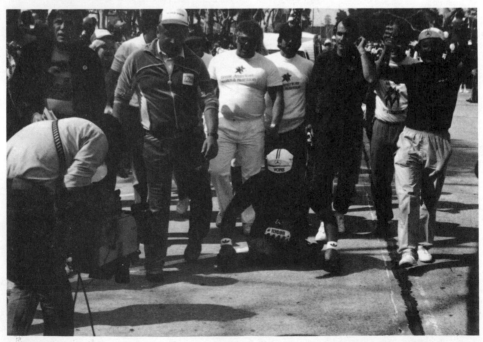

At the L.A. Marathon in 1987, with coach Harry Sneider on left

A year later at the 1988
L.A. Marathon

In his role as Johnny
Skates on NBC/
Stephen Cannell
Television series
Sonny Spoon, with
the star of the
show, Mario Van
Peeples

Bob Wieland, patriot and hero—an inspiration to us all

19
SUMMING UP

The walk wasn't over until I had laid a wreath at the Vietnam wall, to pay respects to the 58,022 men and women killed or missing in action in Southeast Asia. As I took my hands off the wreath, I knew I was laying to rest a part of my own life.

At the ceremony I said, "Here ends the 2,784.1-mile journey, and I just want to praise the Lord for giving Marshall and me the strength to make it this far, and I thank God for the support of the American people all along the journey. We're ending the walk at Wall Twenty-two West, Line Forty-seven, because here is the name of Jerome Lubeno, the young man I did my best to save. Also with me today are Dennis Cooper, who carried me to the helicopter the day I got hit, David Denier, our point man, and Lieutenant Jim Sylvester, my immediate commanding officer. So at this time I think it only fitting that we have a moment of silence."

I wanted the ceremony to be brief and simple, and several people later told me how moving it had been—like the stark wall itself.

Marshall and I held a press conference afterward, answering every imaginable question reporters wanted to ask. And just hours later Marshall and I were on a plane bound for Winnipeg, Manitoba, Canada, to keep some scheduled speak-

ing engagements at Full Gospel Businessmen's meetings and
Strive for Success assemblies. Our good-byes to Jim, David,
Dennis, Paul, Margaret, and everyone else who had come to
support us weren't sad, though I wished I'd had more time.
Even the good-byes were full of victory. I hugged my mom and
dad with a special thank-you. By now my parents were used to
"good-bye, till we meet again."

I had been on the road three years, eight months, and six
days. I had covered approximately five miles per day and
walked a total of 4,900,016 steps—part of which had been
sponsored (at five dollars a step) by individuals I'd met along
the way. For the most part, the people who supported the
Spirit of America were from the grass-roots level. I had
expected to raise a minimum of five dollars per step to feed the
physically hungry and homeless. I was able to contribute a
major portion of the fees I received from many of my speaking
engagements.

The Spirit of America raised up into six figures to feed the
hungry, and we distributed this money through such nonprofit
organizations as the American Red Cross and World Vision.

Moreover, during this period in American history more
money was raised to feed the hungry than ever before. Many
of the people I met along the way considered me one of the
many catalysts for the avalanche of money-raising media
events concerned with the issue of hunger, including We Are
the World, Band Aid, Live Aid, and Farm Aid.

During our Canadian tour we got the news that Americans
who cared about the hungry had formed a human chain
stretching 4,150 miles through sixteen states. People had held
hands to raise money to help feed the physically hungry of
America. Even President Reagan had joined the more than 20
million Americans in 266 cities who had cared enough about
others to give time, money, and energy to the Hands Across
America campaign.

Marshall and I knew that in our own way we had played our
part in calling attention to the plight of the hungry in America.
Even more importantly, scores of spiritually hungry people
came to the Lord as He worked through our witness.

How spiritually hungry America is! It is my earnest prayer that all the lives we touched along the way will grow in Jesus Christ, that their lights will shine and reach thousands of other people's lives. Every Christian is called to witness. I believe America is getting ready for the greatest revival of all time. But for such a revival to occur, it is the responsibility of all Christians to study the Word daily, to spend quiet time with God, and to witness to those who don't know the greatest person who ever lived—Jesus Christ.

Those three years and eight months were historic in other ways as well. America—and the world—had changed. Those were the early years of the new Reagan administration, Grenada had been invaded, and Prince Charles and Lady Di were married. In November of 1984, the Vietnam sculpture by Frederick Hart was unveiled. This statue, dipicting three service men, was placed not far from the controversial wall and was later dedicated by the President before a crowd of one and a half million people.

I also remember that dark moment in our history when the space shuttle *Challenger* exploded on January 28, 1985, and President Reagan reminded us all, "The future doesn't belong to the faint hearted. It belongs to the brave."

It was a period when America was still struggling to extract itself from its history of racial prejudice. Jackey and I rejoiced when the Reverend Martin Luther King's birthday was declared a national holiday. I knew that I wanted to emulate many of the principles that Rev. King had stood for, especially that before there can be peace in the world, people must find peace within their own hearts.

I could look back with amazement at all the natural disasters that had taken place—the earthquake in Coalinga, California, in May 1983 that measured 6.5 on the Richter scale; and the record-breaking cold wave of December of that same year, with its wind-chill factors as low as 100 degrees below zero. More than 800 barges and 80 tugboats were frozen in 8-inch ice on the Mississippi. Then there were the tornados of June 1984 that killed more than a hundred people in the Midwest. I was fortunate to have avoided these disasters, but I prayed daily for the families of the people who had been hurt or killed.

Now that my trip was over, I could look back. I could get some perspective on all that had happened. The world had grown a little bit older, and so had I.

The end of the walk, however, was by no means the end of my story or of my striving for new challenges and goals. In September 1986, Sarah Nichols, the writer we had met in California, called again. She had prayed for me throughout the walk and had even felt led to turn on the TV one day—just in time to see me taking my last steps at the Vietnam wall.

In early October 1986, after much prayer, we agreed that Sarah would write my life story and a film. We celebrated our partnership with a glass of iced tea at the Good Earth Restaurant in Pasadena. On October 6, I rejoiced with Sarah at the birth of her first granddaughter, Summer Lynn Hubbell—a baby that represented to me a new generation of Americans—the hope of the future.

That fall I trained hard for the November 6 New York Marathon. Fred LeBow, president of the New York Marathon, arranged for first-class media coverage, including several of the network morning interview shows.

Those New Yorkers cheered me on—through wind and rain. I finished last, and yet thousands of supporters welcomed me as I crossed the line. One spectator said, however, "Why did you even bother? You finished last!"

"To my way of thinking," I replied, "I finished before the millions of Americans who didn't even take the first step."

"Right on, man," cheered my supporters.

That race began a new phase of my athletic career. I continued a heavy Strive for Success speaking schedule, and before I knew it, I was getting ready for the Los Angeles Marathon in March 1987.

I was chosen by Dr. Bill Burke and the marathon committee to lead off the opening ceremonies for the race. I started three days early, and again, people lined the streets. Paul Beutell came out from the east coast. Sarah walked over thirteen miles with me, which was a miracle in itself, since after her auto accident years before, she hadn't been able to walk very well.

Some Vietnam veterans and their families also walked with me, providing plenty of company.

With my early start, I finished about the same time as the rest of the runners. As I ran toward the finish line, I heard people shout, "Go, Bob, go!" Their enthusiasm gave me an added burst of energy. I was so grateful to take that last step, crossing the line.

After countless more Strive for Success assemblies all over the United States, it was time to train for the 1987 New York Marathon. Back to my old training routines—southern California beaches and up the incline of Santa Anita Boulevard. In November 1987, when I finished the marathon, close to ten thousand New Yorkers cheered me over the line. Someone shouted, "Hey, Bob, *you* should have won the Mercedes!"

On returning, I learned that an executive from Stephen J. Cannell's office had seen me on the ABC "Wide World of Sports" coverage of the NYC Marathon. He asked me to come in and read for the part of Johnny Skates on "Sonny Spoon," Stephen Cannell's new NBC television series starring Mario Van Pebbles. At first I was reluctant; the part was that of a derelict panhandler who used bad language. I couldn't compromise my beliefs and said so to the television executives. They listened. My part was rewritten. I thought of my friend Isaac who years before had urged me to consider an acting career.

That winter, my training associate Harry Sneider and I returned to my home town of Greenfield, Wisconsin, to be honored at "Bob Wieland Day" by the city officials and townspeople. I was deeply moved by the honor given me by the people at Greenfield.

My parents accompanied me to a Strive for Success assembly at my old high school. I had a reunion with Coach Trotalli, my old football coach, and many of my other teachers and schoolmates. My dad could have passed for a lighthouse—he beamed so much joy. It was contagious.

Jackey and I still live in southern California. Pee Wee, our aged attack terrier, is still with us, but Colonel and Sugar have died. Sometimes I think Pee Wee still looks around for Colonel, hoping to attack him.

I recently completed the Iron Man 1988 Triathlon in Kona, Hawaii—the fulfillment of a dream planted in my mind years ago by Dennis Estabrook, who cheered me through the grueling race, along with Geary Whiting my training associate, Marty Slimak, Paul Beutell, and the rest of the team. I swam in the ocean for 2.4 miles, rode a specially designed bike 112 miles, then ran 26 miles.

Marshall married on January 6, 1989, and I rejoiced with him and his new wife, Rose Niemeyer. Isaac Ruiz, his wife, Francine, and their children now live in Phoenix, where he preaches the gospel and acts on television every chance he gets. Tom Damato lives in Thousand Oaks, California, where he teaches computer skills to people from low-income families to help them find work. Our team is spread far and wide, but we will always remember our great adventure.

For all this and more, I praise the Lord Jesus Christ. He is my power source. And whether the finish line is at the end of a cinder track or at the gates of heaven, the race is only run one step at a time.

And He has been with me—every step of the way.

ABOUT THE AUTHORS

Bob Wieland is well-known to many Americans, most notably for his role on NBC's weekly series *Sonny Spoon* and for his appearance on ABC's *Wide World of Sports*, which spotlighted his phenomenal athletic achievements. Bob has changed the lives of thousands of high school students through his motivational "Strive for Success" program. He recently received the 1989 Victory Award and the 1989 Healthiest American Award. He lives with his wife in Arcadia, California.

Sarah Nichols is a professional author and script writer. She wrote *Nature Spirit Connection* and co-wrote *Dr. Bieler's Natural Way to Health*. She has also written films for CBS television and Walt Disney Studios. Most notable is her adaption for film of the Newbery-Award-winning book *Julie of the Wolves* by Jean Craighead George. She has written and produced many scripts for educational video.